A Master Teacher in Canberra for 15 years, Frank McKone trained in educational and community drama under Anton Witsel CAL OAM. He is an honorary life member of the ACT Drama Association and was instrumental in constructing the constitution of the National Association for Drama in Education. He was closely associated with the establishment of The Jigsaw Company, Canberra, and his play *The Death of Willy* was workshopped at the Australian National Playwrights Conference 1981. Admitted as a Fellow of the Australian College of Education in 1986 for 'leadership in drama education as an outstanding teacher and through contributions to course development and teacher in-service education', Frank is now retired from teaching, and is an occasional theatre reviewer for *The Canberra Times*.

Saskai Smith and Darren Schnase in the NIDA production of *Goodnight Children Everywhere* by Richard Nelson, directed by Helmut Bakaitis. (Photo by Branco Gaica, courtesy of NIDA)

# FIRST AUDITION

How to get into drama school

FRANK McKONE

Currency Press, Sydney

First published in 2002 by
Currency Press Pty Ltd
PO Box 2287
Strawberry Hills NSW 2012
www.currency.com.au
enquiries@currency.com.au

Copyright © Frank McKone 2002

Copying for Educational Purposes:
The Australian *Copyright Act* 1968 allows a maximum of one chapter or 10% of this book, whichever is the greater, to be copied by any educational institution for its educational purposes provided that the educational institution (or the body that administers it) has given a remuneration notice to Copyright Agency Limited (CAL) under the Act. For details of the CAL licence for educational institutions please contact CAL, 19/157 Liverpool Street, Sydney, NSW 2000, tel (02) 9394 7600, fax (02) 9394 7601, email: info@copyright.com.au.

Copying for Other Purposes:
Except as permitted under the Act, for example a fair dealing for the purposes of study, research, criticism or review, no part of this book may be reproduced, stored in a retrieval system, or transmitted in any form or by any means without prior written permission. All inquiries should be made to the publisher at the above address.

NATIONAL LIBRARY OF AUSTRALIA CIP DATA
McKone, Frank.
   First audition : how to get into drama school.
   ISBN 0 86819 663 0.
   1. Acting - Study and teaching - Australia. 2. Acting -
   Auditions. I. Title.
792.028071

Cover design by Kate Florance
Printed by Hyde Park Press, Richmond, SA

This book is dedicated to Rupert.

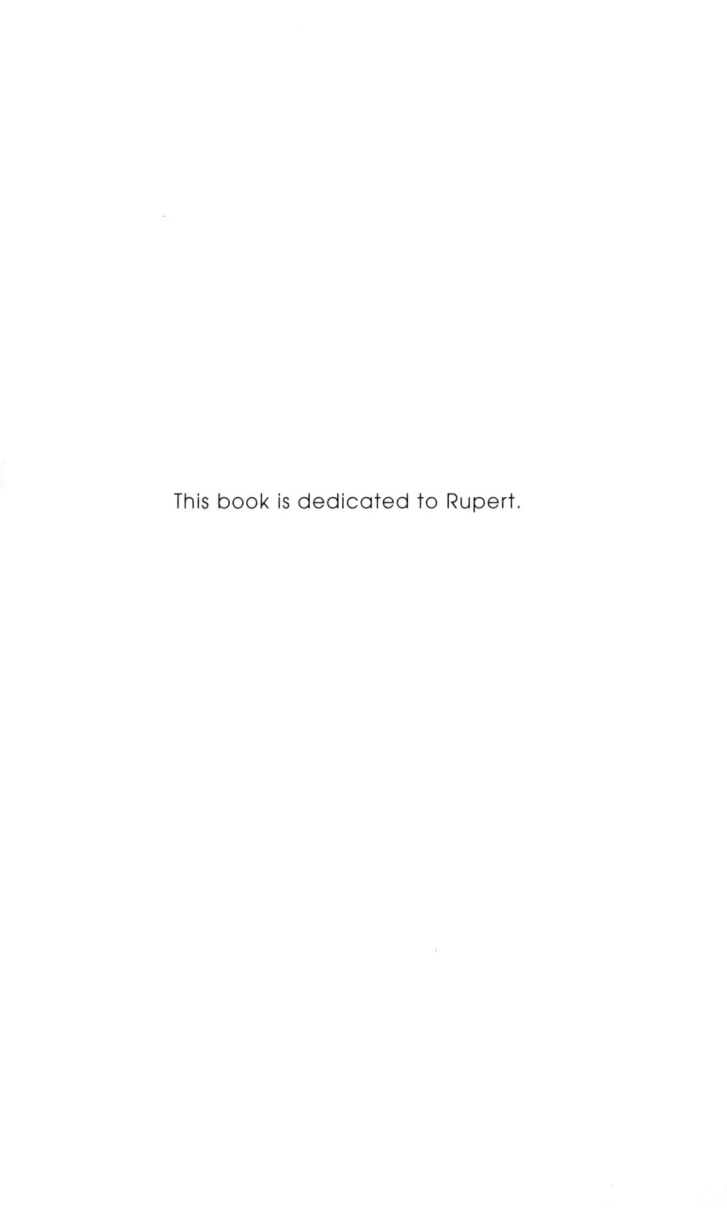

# ACKNOWLEDGEMENTS

Among many professional colleagues, I thank particularly Alanna Maclean, Carol Woodrow and Peter Wilkins who have been for so long the people I could turn to for ideas and criticism; and especially my mentor Anton Witsel whose teaching turned my amorphous enthusiasm into an organised understanding of the processes of drama education.

Excerpt from *A Doll's House* from *A Doll's House and Other Plays* by Henrik Ibsen, translated by Peter Watts (Penguin Books, 1965) copyright © Peter Watts, 1965, reproduced by permission of Penguin Books Ltd.

Excerpt from *After the Fall* copyright © 1964, 1968 by Arthur Miller. Reproduced by permission of the author c/o Rogers, Coleridge & White Ltd., 20 Powis Mews, London W11 1JN in association with International Creative Management, New York.

Excerpt from *The Caucasian Chalk Circle* by Bertolt Brecht, (Methuen, 1984) reproduced by kind permission of Methuen Publishing Limited.

Excerpt from *A Hard God* © Peter Kenna, reproduced by permission of Currency Press.

Excerpt from *Coralie Lansdowne Says No* © Alex Buzo, reproduced by permission of Currency Press.

Excerpt from *Luck of the Draw* © Rosemary John, reproduced by permission of Currency Press.

Excerpt from *The Chapel Perilous* © Dorothy Hewett, reproduced by permission of Currency Press.

# CONTENTS

| | |
|---|---|
| INTRODUCTION | 1 |
| ACT 1: Confrontation with Your Self | 7 |
|    Scene 1: Welcome | 7 |
|    Scene 2: Your physical self | 13 |
| ACT 2: Group and Pair Work | 21 |
|    Scene 1: Group movement and improvisation | 21 |
|    Scene 2: Improvisation and script in pairs | 25 |
| ACT 3: Script Analysis Techniques | 32 |
|    Scene 1: A change of pace | 32 |
|    Scene 2: Sounds and 'syllaphones' | 33 |
|    Scene 3: Beats and Pauses | 41 |
|    Scene 4: Through-lines | 51 |
|    Scene 5: Shakespeare, Shaw and Brecht | 64 |
|    Scene 6: Research | 94 |
| ACT 4: The Audition | 99 |
|    Scene 1: Warming up | 99 |
|    Scene 2: Taking the stage | 102 |
|    Scene 3: The introduction | 106 |
|    Scene 4 : Transition from yourself to your role | 114 |
|    Scene 5: Dramatic shape and audience reaction | 115 |
|    Scene 6: Finish and exit | 117 |
|    Scene 7: Call back and interviews | 119 |
|    Scene 8: Postmortem | 126 |
| APPENDIX: ACT 5 Epilogue | 129 |
| REFERENCES | 147 |

# EXERCISES

| | |
|---|---|
| Exercise 1: Who are you? | 10 |
| Exercise 2: What roles are you physically suited to? | 15 |
| Exercise 3: Warming up | 21 |
| Exercise 4: Doing the random walk | 23 |
| Exercise 5: Skit | 26 |
| Exercise 6: Body language and emotional expression | 27 |
| Exercise 7: Verbal dexterity | 27 |
| Exercise 8: Action in a setting | 27 |
| Exercise 9: Script work with a partner | 29 |
| Exercise 10: Seeing both sides | 31 |
| Exercise 11: Syllaphones # 1 | 34 |
| Exercise 12: Syllaphones #2 | 35 |
| Exercise 13: Syllaphones #3 | 39 |
| Exercise 14: Beats and pauses #1 | 43 |
| Exercise 15: Beats and pauses in *Coralie Lansdowne Says No* | 48 |
| Exercise 16: Beats and pauses in *Furtive Love* | 49 |
| Exercise 17: Mother, I'm home | 51 |
| Exercise 18: Through-lines: response to self | 54 |
| Exercise 19: Through-lines: response to the other | 59 |
| Exercise 20: Through-lines: response to self and the other | 62 |
| Exercise 21: Syllaphones in Shakespeare | 68 |
| Exercise 22: The pentameter | 71 |
| Exercise 23: The caesura | 73 |
| Exercise 24: Emotional through-lines in Shakespeare | 74 |
| Exercise 25: Objectives analysis in Shakespeare | 76 |

| | |
|---|---|
| Exercise 26: Audience response analysis in Shaw | 83 |
| Exercise 27: Creating the effect in Shaw | 84 |
| Exercise 28: Shaping the character in Shaw | 86 |
| Exercise 29: Syllaphones, beats, pauses and stress patterns in Brecht | 88 |
| Exercise 30: Reversal words in Brecht | 90 |
| Exercise 31: Singing the song in Brecht | 91 |
| Exercise 32: Naturalism | 93 |
| Exercise 33: Warm-up exercise | 101 |
| Exercise 34: Taking the stage | 103 |
| Exercise 35: The announcement | 112 |
| Exercise 36: Test of knowledge | 125 |
| Exercise 37: Written presentation | 125 |
| Exercise 38: Oral presentation | 126 |

Tammy Clarkson and Nicholas Davies in the WAAPA production of *In Our Town*. (Photo by Peter Northcott, courtesy of WAAPA)

# INTRODUCTION

I assume you've bought this book because you need to prepare for an audition by yourself, or perhaps you want to add to your practical experience. I would have preferred to be with you in person while you take this course and, although a book on how to do drama is never as good as the real thing, I'll do my best for you. In this book I will describe a range of training activities and exercises that will prepare you for your audition. Remember that in drama you learn by doing: don't just read the exercises, *do* them.

Before we begin, you must think carefully about sort of course you are most suited to. In Australia, there are many different kinds of training courses. Some of the options are:

- university courses in which drama/theatre/media units are part of a general degree course (this means you take other academic courses at the same time);
- university courses in performing arts (which means you can make up almost all your program with units in drama/theatre/media);
- university training courses in theatre—including the National Institute for Dramatic Art (NIDA), the Victorian College of the Arts (VCA) or the Western Australian Academy for Performing Arts (WAAPA)—which are designed to turn out professional commercially employable actors, technicians, stage craft workers, stage managers and directors;
- university courses for training to become a teacher in performing arts in primary or secondary schools;

- Technical and Further Education (TAFE) courses in drama / theatre, including training in specialist stage crafts and technical work;
- private training courses, usually concentrating on acting;
- private skills classes, usually specialising in aspects of acting (like voice, singing, movement, fencing, dance).

Most of the university level courses are competitive entry, and are open to all-comers. The selection process varies between courses. Some institutions will require an audition and an interview, while others will rely entirely on your final Year 12 results. Some courses prefer the students to be at least 20 years of age before applying, which would mean that you would be competing with people who may have much more extensive theatre experience than you. More information is given on the requirements of different institutions in Act 5: Epilogue.

This book will give you the techniques and skills that will be required if you are going to audition for university-level training. Of course, I am unable to guarantee your success—even if you are very, very good, the competition and special needs of some courses means you may not be accepted.

I hope that this book will help you clarify your picture of yourself, and that you will be able to identify your personal strengths and weaknesses, as well as your skills. You may find that, as your self-awareness grows, your aims change as you work through the book. You may even decide that theatre is not the right way to go for you.

If you are in your final year of high school or

college, make sure you put in applications for a range of courses at several different institutions, including courses that don't require auditions—it is always best to leave yourself as many options as possible. Consider taking courses interstate or away from your local region as it's often good to gain experience in a different setting.

If you are a young adult or more mature person already experienced in theatre, I hope my book will add to your techniques and understandings.

I have found that there is a common view that raw talent will get you through an audition, and that talent is all you need to get through a training course. I don't think that this is the truth. I've seen too many people drop out of (or be dropped out of) theatre training courses, despite their talents. This has happened for many different reasons, but the first has usually been that they got through the audition without being thoroughly prepared. In a sense, their talent got them through on false pretences. If you are to be successful in an audition, you need to rely on more than luck. You should be able to feel that your success is justified because you are ready for training both *personally* (being clear-minded and committed), and *technically* (having knowledge and skills).

You may want to work through this book because you need new ideas and techniques for when you audition for parts. While I have written this book specifically for school-leavers and young adults, the exercises in this book would be beneficial for good amateur and semi-professional (and perhaps the occasional professional) audition.

Finally, you may be more interested in the technical

or management side of theatre, such as lighting, sound, costumes, make-up, sets, stage management, front of house management, production management, directing. You too will need to understand what is required of an actor, and your knowledge of what is required will help you get into training. In some cases, all applicants (whether for acting or non-acting courses) are taken through group activities, maybe some pair work, perhaps an individual acting audition and an interview (in which the technical specialist may be required to present a design, a folio of work, and often an essay explaining their approach to the industry).

The work of an actor is very much dependent upon the competency of the technical and management staff. Because the actor is the centre of the audience's attention and faces the direct response from the audience, everyone in the team must understand what the actor is doing. Actors, of course, must also understand what the other people in the team are doing.

If you have experienced tension in a theatre production, you may have noticed that it often stems from a demarcation dispute between the different departments. Theatrical production is exciting partly because of this tension—it really is difficult to have such a diverse group of specialists work so well together that a performance becomes a wonderful experience for perhaps thousands of people in the audience. Achieving such unity in diversity is your professional aim.

This book will help each of you be as well-prepared as possible before that very special audience: the auditioner.

## A note for theatre teachers

This book records some of the methods I use and have found to be successful. Maybe you will find some of my ideas a bit quirky and perhaps one or two a bit risky. Theatre is a creative and individual process: please use what you will from my approach. I hope you will have many other ideas to add to mine.

Joseph Manning and Jenny Schwinghammer in the VCA production of *The Rover*. (Photo: Jeff Busby)

# ACT 1
# Confrontation with your self

## SCENE 1
## Welcome

When you arrive at my class, you walk into a large open space. The studio has been emptied of furniture except for a few seats along one side, placed in the centre of the wall. All the working lights are on so that there are no highlights or darker areas. You will find me in the central seat. Other people may have already arrived, some sitting to my left, some to my right. Perhaps you are the last to arrive. You will be the sixth person and you are invited to take the empty seat on my left.

My class won't have more than six people because the work is quite intense and individualised. Each of you will go through the same set of experiences one by one. Normally we work in three hour sessions: it usually takes about half an hour for each person to go through the first confrontation with your self.

As you read this book, try to act as you would if you were in the living studio. I have written this book as if I am speaking directly to you, and you can imagine me in my seat talking. You'll see a short red-bearded person with glasses and a bald head. My face is roundish with a slightly bobbly nose and fairly deep-set eyes, which are brown towards hazel. There are smile-creases around my eyes and my cheek-bones are quite high and would be more prominent except that my full beard covers most of the details.

My speaking voice is quiet. You will often have to

listen carefully to be sure of what I've said. I pitch my voice around my natural note which is a baritone, without deep resonances unless I deliberately seek out a bass effect. My voice varies in pitch much more than you at first may realise, often going up to a light tenor.

Sometimes I seem to direct my gaze directly into your eyes. This is often when I have set up an expectation for you to do something and you haven't taken the initiative. At other times my gaze seems to wander off to the side for a while, as if I am wondering about what I should say next. This opens up an opportunity for you to reflect for a while on what has just happened, how you feel about the experience, and to gather your thoughts together ready for the next step. These are moments when you might put in a comment or ask a question. Or perhaps everyone feels that the moment should be left in silence.

Let's begin.

I spend some time seeking out your background experience. What have you been doing in drama in the past year or two? What sort of shows have you performed in? What did you think of the director of the show you most enjoyed being in? Have you tried to direct some drama yourself? There are many questions.

I spread the questions around the group, often looking aside while someone speaks. What I want to know is how much people know about theatre. Does Vivienne, who has told us that she has often had lead roles in musicals, see herself in a blinkered way or does she seem to be open to working in different ways in different productions? Does Tom's apparent technical expertise in lighting mean that he's not really sensitive to other people's feelings? Susan is obviously intelligent in an academic way, but has she also kept a sense of simple joy in her acting and an open kind of enthusiasm? Paul makes his fear of writing essays very obvious, but his enthusiasm about rehearsing and developing characters shows his intelligence.

Remember that you are preparing yourself for professional training which will hopefully take you on to a career which will always demand your energy and commitment, and in which you can never rest on your laurels. Finding work is always a risky business. You will need to learn how to balance the dedication and total focus required if you are to work in the theatre industry, against your commitments to people and life outside the theatre.

If you do not know, even in your imagination, what I mean, then it is time to reconsider your intentions. Spend some time getting to know the theatre scene in your town. Set up a work experience placement backstage or in theatre administration. Interview theatre workers and seek out information about how they cope, what their work conditions are like, how the trade unions operate.

Maybe this means delaying the time to audition. Many of my successful students have not auditioned as soon as they have completed school, but have spent a year or two working (at any kind of job to support themselves) and doing the kind of hands-on research I suggest. Some have helped a professional director as a director's assistant; some have found small-scale work backstage as a dresser or helping to operate sound or lights. Some have spent a year reading plays and theatre history. Some have gone to uni to do an arts or teaching or science or some other degree, before finding themselves ready for the serious business of theatre.

But here you are, ready for your first exercise. Make sure you do the exercise before reading ahead.

## EXERCISE 1: WHO ARE YOU?

All you need is an ordinary room with plenty of space in the centre. Place a chair in the middle of one side of the space. That's where I sit. (You could set up a video camera to represent me, if you like.)

I will give you the very simple instruction: 'Come towards us to a point where you think you should stop, and tell us who you are'. That's all the instructions that I will give you.

Go to the opposite side, turn and come towards the chair. Choose where to stop, and tell the imaginary me *who you are...*

How did you go? What did you do? What did you say? Write down everything you remember (and what you can see, if you made a video) about your body movements from the moment you began to turn towards the chair, through to some seconds after you finished speaking.

Record as much as you can about your head movements, your eye movements, your hand movements, your legs and feet. How were you breathing as you turned, as you walked, as you spoke, after you finished speaking?

Write down exactly what you said, including how you said it. Record any slight hesitations, how soft or how loud, how precisely you articulated words, how fast or slow, how flat (monotone) or lively (varied intonation).

Also write down exactly how you felt at each point of the exercise: turning, walking, speaking, after speaking. Make sure you record your feelings (such as elated, anxious, terrible, confident) rather than your thoughts (such as 'I thought this was a peculiar exercise').

Now we begin the confrontation with your self. Make sure that you are as honest with yourself as possible. Look over everything you wrote down, and ask yourself whether you presented your real self. Did you cover up some aspects of yourself, either deliberately or because you were nervous or embarrassed? Were there any signs, in your body movements, tone of voice, or what you said, that would indicate that you weren't being completely open about yourself?

Did you, for example, turn and walk quickly, stop abruptly and say 'Hello, I'm Sally' in a way that might have looked aggressive because you wanted to create the impression that you are much more confident than you really are?

Or did you turn deliberately slowly, toss your hair back, and stroll forward and take an easy loose position while saying 'Hi, my name's Robert', because you wanted to appear cool and sophisticated when really that's an act you have tended to put on since about Year 9.

Maybe you stood up quite close to say 'I'm Melanie and I hope to become a professional actor one day', and only when you look back on this do you realise that you were not giving the imaginary person in the chair much breathing space and they would have felt dominated by you; or maybe you came across as making some kind of sexual proposition which you didn't really intend.

In my classes I ask the people who have watched you 'Do you think you saw the real Sally/Robert/Melanie?' As we discuss—in front of you—what we think, I ask people to distinguish between deliberate covering up of facets of your self, and things you do which are habits or normal given the circumstances. In my examples, Sally may have walked quickly as she was nervous, Robert may have deliberately tossed his hair back, and Melanie's 'proposition' may be a habit. The people watching you are normally able to distinguish which is which.

As you are working alone and don't have other people to give you feedback, you must consider these examples and your own responses. If you have used a video camera, watch the tape as though you are one of your classmates. This may help you be more objective in your answers. Isolate the areas of your presentation that disguise your real self, and work hard to eliminate them so that the auditioner will see you as you really are.

The auditioners are very experienced at observing people and will choose students who will be good to work with, who are open to suggestions, who are aware of their own feelings and how other people perceive them. If they see ingrained habits or deliberate attempts to manipulate them, they will know they will have to spend a lot of time in the training classes eliminating habits and making you more flexible emotionally.

It is really important that you are clear about the difference between when you are being yourself and when you are acting. Reading Stanislavsky or Benedetti or Hayes Gordon (see Act 5: Epilogue: References) can help, but the crunch is that you have to examine yourself and know that you know the difference. Acting often involves expressing the emotions a character would feel. For your own peace of mind you need to be sure that you can act 'as if' without getting confused about who you are.

## SCENE 2
### Your physical self

We will now deal with another important aspect of confronting your self. We'll start by having a careful look at me, and I will ask you questions about what you see.

You see a male in his sixties, though some think he doesn't look as old as that. He is short, with slightly bowed legs and a small pot tummy. His shoulders are fairly even. His chin is emphasised by his beard, most of which is red but with a lighter section, now beginning to go grey in the front. His nose is not aquiline but has a quite significant bump halfway down and slightly flared nostrils. His cheekbones are actually quite flat but are made more prominent by his deep-set eyes. His eyes are, as a result, not easily accessible unless he deliberately widens them. His forehead is quite wide, fairly high (especially because most of his head is bald) and has few wrinkles, but there are laugh lines around his eyes. His ears are quite prominent. His general build is lightweight but looks a bit stocky because he is short.

This description is not all that can be observed, of course, but this is enough to begin to ask the next questions.

If this person were auditioning for a training course which included film and television work, would his physical features help or hinder?

One answer may be that the deep-set eyes and flat cheekbones may not work well in film. It is possible to effectively alter these features with make-up for stage work, but it would not be possible to disguise them in film close ups.

If this person were auditioning for a training course aimed at producing commercial star actors, how would he go?

The answer is, not very well. He is not tall enough to take lead roles, especially working with women who are likely to be taller than him.

Are there particular parts which it would be difficult to cast him in, or parts where he could be easily type-cast?

Answer: it's unlikely that anyone would cast him as Hamlet, unless the director was a bit quirky and wanted to turn Hamlet's self-obsession into an attitude caused by his small and unathletic body, or perhaps wanted to re-create the actual heights of people in the Middle Ages (which would mean using all short people according to modern standards).

This person's general demeanour and effect on stage tends towards the comic rather than the conventional idea of the tragic. Characters in farce, clown-type characters are therefore the type-cast (and in fact these were the parts I used to play); but it is then possible to see other parts (for example, one of the tramps in Samuel Beckett's *Waiting for Godot*) in which the outward characteristics appear comic while tragedy is the reality for the character's inner life.

# EXERCISE 2: WHAT ROLES ARE YOU PHYSICALLY SUITED TO?

Set up a full length mirror on one side of an empty space. Go to the opposite side of the space and walk slowly towards the mirror, stopping a metre or so short of it. As you walk and for a considerable time after you stop, observe as objectively as you can all the details of your physical features.

Write down a complete description of your physical self in the third person (he has / she has). Then ask yourself about:

- film and television work
- unlikely roles
- type-cast roles
- interesting roles

You should now be keeping a regular diary of all your drama experiences, and in it you should record your responses to the exercises in this book. You will find it fascinating to compare your ideas about yourself at this point in your career with what actually happens.

Remember as you confront your self that it is impossible to predict with any accuracy what will happen in the future. Maybe there is a particular niche in film and television for you that you haven't considered. What you thought were unlikely roles may be the ones you get as directors and audiences change their ideas about theatre. You may want to avoid type-casting, but perhaps these sorts of roles can become your bread-and-butter, paying your wages while you try for more interesting roles. On the other hand, always keep looking for the interesting roles: these are the ones which will challenge you and test your

Joseph Manning and Sibylla Budd in the 1998 VCA production of *Lover's Meeting*. (Photo: Jeff Busby)

skills, and through which you will grow as a professional performer.

You have confronted yourself in two different ways in these exercises. You've had it easy compared with those who physically attend my classes. As you stand there and hear the other people's descriptions of your physical features, your apparent attitudes and the emotional effects you create in them, you may realise some important things about yourself, things you will need to know if you hope to become a theatre worker.

An important thing to remember is that different people will perceive and respond to you in different ways. It isn't often that all five people come up with the same observations about you. This is a good thing to know. You never need to assume that everyone thinks of you in the same way. When you are auditioning, for example, you need not be terribly down after one auditioner has rejected you for a training course or a particular part. This auditioner has to make a decision to try to find the 'right' person for the situation as the auditioner sees it. When you go for the next audition, the situation is different, and the auditioner is different. Remember that rejections are not rejections of you, but are statements that this particular auditioner felt that you wouldn't be suitable for a particular production, or course.

As you gain experience, you will become more familiar with different auditioners and the nature of the situations they are interested in. In the case of training and higher education courses, you may be surprised at how different they are in each university.

Catherine, a former student, writes 'I did, in fact,

get accepted into [University of …]. It ended up that my TER was a factor—something they did not tell us anything about'. Her belief that she had been rejected when she auditioned turned out to be only part of the story. She went on to become a full-time professional technical and production manager.

Anne, some years before, seemed to romp through the audition for another university and gained very good results in her first year. Halfway through her second year I met her back in her home town. She told me 'I didn't like their approach, I found them too clinical and they didn't seem interested in real creative work. I'm going to run drama-based holiday programs for young children and I'm putting in a portfolio to get into art school next year'. Which she did, and formed her own multimedia theatre.

Nigel, in a different year, had gone to the same university course. When I met him a year and a half later, he had been advised that he would be better off not attempting the next semester. He had reached the same conclusion, saying that although he had skills which had seemed suitable at the audition, he had not been able to build on them and he probably wasn't ready for the demands of theatre work. By this time he had discovered a new interest in naturopathy, did an appropriate training course and set up in his own business.

These anecdotes can be multiplied by the number of people who have been through my classes. Life is ever-changing and it is important that you consider the different options available to you in your future career. Rejection at auditions can be devastating for the person who has only one possibility in mind.

It is also important for you to remember that your experiences will change you, and as your career progresses you may find your goals changing. Perhaps you will have noticed after attempting these exercises that your feelings are already more open and, if you try the first exercise again, you present your real self more naturally and easily than before. If this is happening it is a good sign, and indicates that you will be able to adapt your presentation in a sincere way for different audition situations. This should open up more opportunities for you.

Training for auditions can never guarantee you success—but learning to confront your self in a positive way can certainly help.

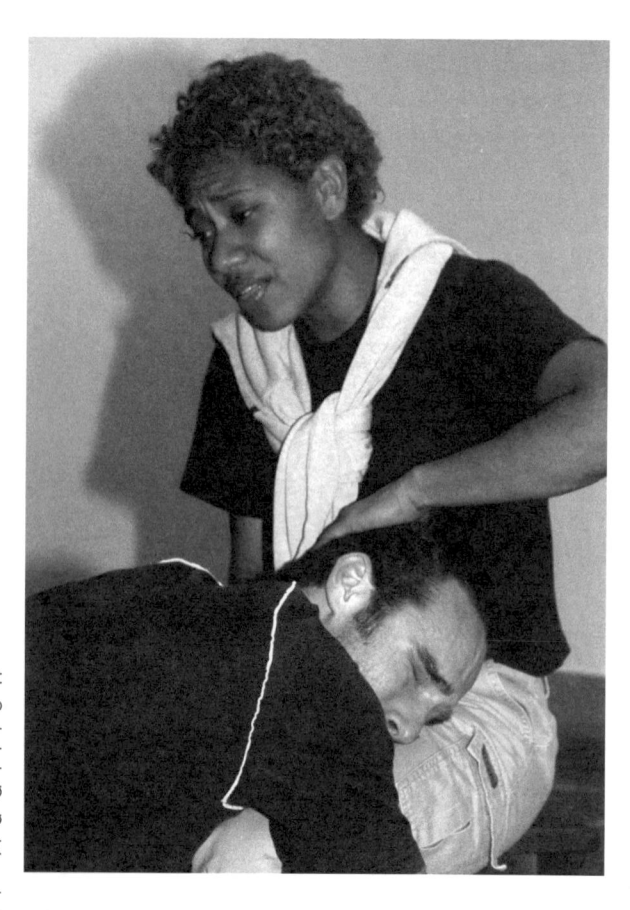

Winston Cooper and Lynette Bennett in rehearsal for the QUT production of *Art of Success*, directed by John O'Hare. (Photo: Ben MacMahon)

# ACT 2
# Group and pair work

## SCENE 1
## Group movement and improvisation

Now, in a group—even with auditioners observing—it's not just you confronting yourself. Working with other people, as in a workshop or rehearsal, means you can enjoy expressing yourself and relate to people. Your audience is not your focus now.

As you are reading this book, without a group to work with, you'll have to use your experience and imagination in the exercises. The activities we will be doing are probably similar to ones you've done before, and could be the sort of work you are asked to do on your audition day.

### EXERCISE 3: WARMING UP

1. Form groups of 3. Stand in a small circle, about 30-40cms across. Place your feet at a slight outward angle, so that each person's toes are almost touching the next person's toes. Bend and stretch, keeping your feet in position (but not necessarily flat on the floor), so that each person lightly touches as many places as possible on their partners' bodies (front and back).

2. Work with a partner about the same height and weight as yourself. Stand facing each other, touching toes, without falling backwards. Gripping your partners' wrists and keeping your bodies straight (no bending at knees or waist), both you and your partner lean back, until you are balanced with arms stretched.

3. With the group in a circle, walk clockwise while keeping step to a strict beat. Keep equidistant from the person ahead and behind and maintain the original size of the circle. At random, your director will increase or slow down the beat and change the group's direction.
4. Loosen up joints and take a parallel stance, with your spine extended and eyes horizontal (centred position). Sense your weight on the floor. Let your body lean away from vertical, putting more weight on your right foot, left foot, balls of your feet and your heels in turn. Take your lean to its limits before you begin to fall. Then take your lean past the limit, begin to fall and, by moving your feet, recover to vertical centred position.
5. Begin in groups of 3, and later move so the whole group is in a circle. Using basic voice warm-up sounds (such as ma-ba, da-ta, na-na, la-la, za-sa, nga-nga) make 'conversation' with your partners.

Each of these exercises can be extended: 1 can be taken into movement improvisation and dance; 2 is a beginning for circus skills and body contact work; 3 tests timing and sense of space (the next step is to break the circle, going on to use music or establishing your own rhythm within the group); 4 works on confidence in your physical movement; and 5 can be extended into full speaking improvisation and singing.

If you were an auditioner watching a group doing these exercises, you would easily be able to judge people's basic physical skills (and therefore who would be more easily trainable). Yet from your point of view, you will most easily succeed in these exercises if you

have had some experience with these kinds of activities—
and if you are able to relax and enjoy doing them.

Were there any parts of the exercises that, as a
group, you were struggling with? Set up a plan of
action to work on the skills that you feel need
improving. Come back to these exercises later, and
discuss, with the group, whether you have improved.

These warming up exercises are also appropriate
for people who would like to get into the technical or
management side of theatre training, as they may have
to work in a combined group before moving into their
specialised courses.

## EXERCISE 4: DOING THE RANDOM WALK

There are literally thousands of exercises which
auditioners may set up to to see how well you focus, how
imaginative you are and how sincere you are in
establishing and maintaining a role. Doing the Random
Walk may be used as a model.

Begin with Warm up Exercise 3. Walk in a circle,
keeping strict time. The director will give instructions in
sidecoaching mode. Keeping a strict time, break out of
the circle and walk at random around the space,
avoiding bumping into other actors.

Working now to your own timing, walk at random with
the objective of keeping equidistant from the other
actors near you. The group should try to fill the entire
space, without making any direct eye contact with each
other.

Once the group can keep this 'random equidistant'
state for a reasonable time (judged by the actors, not
the director), the actors may establish eye contact, but
only briefly as they chance to face someone else.

After most actors have 'met', two actors may establish eye contact and lock for some time, either stopping or keeping the movement going. When they feel ready, they break away from each other.

Once 'contact, lock, and break away' is established, actors may add words which express to the other actor how they feel in the 'lock' stage.

This can then be extended into full conversations, and may develop into contact between more than two actors at a time until it becomes a total group extended improvisation.

The exercise is completed by stepping back to brief eye contact without words, to the random equidistant state, to rhythmic circle, and, finally, rest.

This exercise is designed to leave you with a simple framework for action. You must develop and maintain your own focus, while both reacting to and initiating feelings based upon the body language and expressions you see when you make eye contact.

If you are focussed and allow yourself to receive messages from others, you will find that you develop (at a subliminal level) a kind of 'character' which is not exactly you but that has some of your characteristics. It is this 'character' which begins to speak in the later part of the exercise.

If you are sensitive to your own and other people's feelings, and stay true to the 'character' you develop, you will show an auditioner watching the group that you are ready for more training in acting.

This exercise is specifically for people who intend to train or work as actors. It involves much more delicate work than the warm up exercises, and calls upon your sensitivity and imagination.

How well do you think the group performed as a whole? Were any of the 'characters' that were created habitual or stereotyped? Remember the exercises from Act 1. Through confronting your self you learned that being yourself means not 'putting on an act' for the auditioner. The character that you created in Doing the Random Walk should not 'put on an act' for the other characters it meets either. You are acting a role, but do your best to do so with sincerity.

## SCENE 2
## Improvisation and script in pairs

You have probably already had experience performing skits, short improvisations, and scripted scenes with a partner in drama classes, or when auditioning for parts. What can you expect now you are approaching professional training? More of the same, or something different? There are thousands of exercises the auditioners may ask you to do—I will describe a few that should prepare you for most eventualities. (You may find it useful to come back to these exercises after you have completed Act 3: Script analysis techniques.)

### Skits

A skit is a (usually short) situation or plot-based act. In an audition you will have very limited time to prepare the outline of the plot. It is quite unlikely that auditioners would ask for skits to be performed as it is very difficult not to fall into exaggeration and stereotyping.

However, some of the Theatresports® games could be used, as the constraints of each game focus on skills which an auditioner might wish to see people demonstrate. Space Jump is one such game.

## EXERCISE 5: SKIT

Pairs are given 2 minutes to prepare a 2-minute skit. They are given the following instructions.

- ■ Actor A sets a scene which is clearly understandable to the audience. Speech may be included.
- ■ Actor B enters and responds to the scene as it appears to be.
- ■ Actor A, through the action, shows that the original scene is not as it first appeared to be.
- ■ Actor B, through the action, accepts or rejects the new situation.
- ■ Actors A and B freeze at a strong moment of resolution or conflict.

This exercise places the same constraints on the actors as Space Jump—the shape of the action is predetermined, and both actors must initiate action and work together to produce a strong ending. However, even with little time to prepare, with quick thinking and sensitive actors it is possible to create a strong emotional response in the audience, making this exercise suitable for auditions.

## Improvisation

A good improvisation (like a good naturalistic play) will focus on drama arising from character, rather than situation or plot. It is difficult for an improvisation to work successfully in an audition situation, as actors often need to work together for a certain period of time to establish a relationship that will allow them to improvise confidently together.

However, the following exercises may be used in an audition situation. They all focus on different skills that the auditioners will be looking for.

## EXERCISE 6: BODY LANGUAGE AND EMOTIONAL EXPRESSION

The actors, on opposite sides of the performing space, take a position which expresses a feeling. This could be based on a word given to each one privately by the director. Alternatively the actors may be asked to silently decide for themselves the feeling they will begin with. Without using words, the characters then establish a relationship, and may conclude either when the characters are at a point where they will stay together, or where they break apart and leave.

## EXERCISE 7: VERBAL DEXTERITY

The actors are each given a different word describing an attitude towards the other. The words are designed to create conflict. The words may be announced to the audience. The actors then meet briefly to establish a topic of common interest. The improvisation consists of a 'conversation' about the common interest. The objective of your 'character' is to win by maintaining its attitude while causing the other 'character' to change their attitude.

## EXERCISE 8: ACTION IN A SETTING

The director describes a set and the characters' reasons for being there. For example, the director may lay out a room in the acting space by walking around the perimeter. They may describe the furniture and where it is placed.

The director may tell you, for example: 'It is a bedroom. The door is USL of the fictional room. There is a window opposite, but the curtains are drawn. The bed (USC) is covered with dust sheets. The dressing table

(DSC) has nothing on it but a framed photograph. The instructions are that you both enter the room, as two people who, in the past, have had a relationship with each other and with this room. You are returning for the first time in many years because circumstances have changed and something must now be done.'

You meet briefly with your partner to decide what kind of relationship you had, and enter the room. No decision has been made about what to do. While in the room each feature must be part of the action.

When the characters have reached a decision (even if it is not expressed in so many words) they leave the room. The improvisation must not be longer than 2 minutes.

Although each exercise has a different focus, they all ask you to not only take on a task or a role as an individual, but to also work on the spot with your partner to complete the exercise as if it were a tiny drama.

Your monologue audition is also like a whole play—all in one short speech. Some auditioners will want to see how well you work with others: do you give and take? Do you tend to block? Do you allow your partner to take the lead all the time?

## Script Work

Working with a partner on a short extract from a play without much preparation time will reveal to the auditioners how well you work with others, as well as your ability to translate words on a page into action.

Again, it may be useful to come back to this exercise when you have completed the work in Act 3 —this exercise can be an unfairly bad experience for someone who hasn't previously been trained in script analysis.

Dorothy Hewett's *The Chapel Perilous* is, on the whole, more expressionist than naturalistic, but the following scene from the play is ideal for an audition situation: the brief meeting between Sally and Michael allows the actors to show the varying emotions of both characters. It is also well balanced between the two characters.

## EXERCISE 9: SCRIPT WORK WITH A PARTNER

Actors are usually given 10 minutes in a quiet area off stage to read the script and prepare for the reading. On call, Sally enters and takes her position. Michael enters US from Sally. (It may help to skip ahead to Act 4 Scene 2: Taking the stage and Act 4 Scene 6: Finish and exit before doing this exercise.)

*The Chapel Perilous*
Dorothy Hewett
Currency Press, 1981

SALLY: Workers' Star. Rally for Peace and Freedom.
MICHAEL: (*softly*) Sally.
  *She swings round.*
  I can draw the shape of your face in the dark. Like a heart. And yet there've been times when I couldn't remember ...
SALLY: And that was most of the time.
MICHAEL: It was no use prolonging the agony.
SALLY: Is that what you called it?
MICHAEL: Sally, what did you want, what did you really want?
SALLY: I wanted you to say: 'I love you. Have our baby and we'll go away together.' But you didn't say it, did you?
MICHAEL: If it's any satisfaction, I've missed you.

SALLY: Except when you forgot my face.

MICHAEL: Did you ever think of me?

SALLY: When I saw our baby lying there, a lump of bloody gristle, I thought of you, and I hated you.

    *Pause.*

MICHAEL: (*recovering*) And now you're happy?

SALLY: I had Thomas's baby to replace the one we murdered. And I speak on soap boxes but I never write poetry any more. It's as if I'd turned dumb forever.

    MICHAEL *moves towards her.*

Stay where you are.

MICHAEL: (*triumphantly*) You're afraid, afraid I'll touch you.

    *He laughs, she closes her eyes.*

Go home then, go home to Thomas. Feed your baby, carry your banner, sweet Sister Sally, and never see me again.

    *Her eyes fly open.*

Where's my brave wild girl gone now?

SALLY: You destroyed her.

MICHAEL: She's indestructible, and she wants me still.

SALLY: No.

MICHAEL: What if I was to say I've learnt my lesson, that every girl in every bed was you, every corner I turned in every crummy town I hoped you might be there?

SALLY: Leave me alone, Michael. Please.

MICHAEL: I'll wait for you tonight under the bridge. You'll come. I know you, Sally.

    *He leans closer, careful not to touch her. She stands rigid. He drops a coin in her hand.*

Give us a *Workers' Star.* Funny, you never struck me as a likely recruit to the ranks of the working class, Sal.

As you may have never seen the script before and you have only 10 minutes to prepare, the first thing that you and your partner must consider is what the auditioner is looking for. Is it the perfect rendition of these two characters? Obviously not, with only 10 minutes preparation time. Is it how well the two of you can work together as actors? Obviously yes.

The key to working well on stage is working well off stage and using your 10 minutes preparation time well. Make sure your ideas about staging and character are heard by your partner—and make equally sure you hear your partner's ideas. If you can reach an agreed, give-and-take relationship (even if you haven't worked out all the details about the script) in the 10 minutes off stage, the 2 minutes on stage will go well.

## EXERCISE 10: SEEING BOTH SIDES

Using *The Chapel Perilous*, role-play the 10 minutes before going on stage:
- with yourself as Sally, and your partner as Michael
- with your partner as Sally, and yourself as Michael

To break down sex-role assumptions, do the exercise three times, with mixed-sex and same sex combinations.

You might need an interval now, before the Big One: Act 3—Script analysis techniques.

# ACT 3
# Script analysis techniques

## SCENE 1
## A change of pace

Everything I asked you to do in Act 1: Confrontation with your self is very close to you personally. In Act 2: Group and pair work you were able to relax as you focussed on enjoying the action and your new relationships. Now you are aware that to confront your self you need to observe and be sensitive to how you feel about yourself, as well as try to gauge how other people feel about you. This is never easy, as all actors know, but it's also exciting to work so near to your real feelings: it's what makes acting so satisfying.

As you enter the space today, you will notice that the atmosphere is different. Everyone is friendly and warm now they have all been through the same experiences as you, but the chairs are set up in a circle and I seem to be waiting to speak to the group formally.

The hardest part of being an excellent actor, I think, is that you need to learn so much about technique, yet technique must never dominate over genuine sensitivity to feelings. Act 3 is a long section with a lot of technical exercises, and you will need to be very patient as you work through them. Think of each exercise and the information that goes with it as a new challenge. When you feel a bit daunted by what I ask you to do and learn, put the book away for a while and relax, and come back to the work when you are able to think more clearly.

You may already know some of the information in Act 3, but please don't skip any of the exercises. I have put the information and exercises together in such a way so that you are able to prepare your audition speeches properly. By working through the basics of sounds and the silences between sounds you will give yourself the grounding for the more complex work of giving your speeches meaning, feeling and character in naturalistic plays. Finally you will learn to apply your techniques to the work of three different authors—Shakespeare, Shaw and Brecht. You will be able to adapt the techniques you learn in these exercises to a variety of audition pieces.

## SCENE 2
## Sounds and 'syllaphones'

The study of the sounds of speech is called phonetics. To become a good actor you will need to learn a great deal about phonetics. I will teach you some basic information which you will build on when you take a higher education course.

Understanding the basics of how spoken language works will help in an audition, especially where the auditioner asks you to present a piece in a different way from the way you prepared it. With knowledge, your intuition can work to produce the required effect.

Incidentally, if you have trouble reading and writing, perhaps because of some form of dyslexia, don't worry—using a tape recorder, you will be able to do these exercises audio-aurally instead of visually. You can learn your lines from a tape and then apply the techniques to present them how you want them.

So settle in now for some focussed work on language.

# EXERCISE 11: SYLLAPHONES #1

Read and record the following sentence on a tape recorder:

> Your payment will be processed by Electronic Funds Transfer.

Listen to the tape of your reading very carefully. You will notice that the sentence consists of a series of sounds. Only when they are put together in order do they make sense. Listen to your tape again, and break the sentence down into each of the individual sounds in the series:

> y - o - er - p - eh - m - e - nt ... and so on.

Listen to the tape again, and this time break it down into the natural groupings of sounds (what I call syllaphones). It will probably come out something like:

> yaw peh ment will bi pro sest bai i lek tron ik funds trans fer

Read this back on to the tape. The result, if you keep your voice monotone, is likely to sound rather like a Darlek from the Dr. Who series!

You'll notice that syllaphones are much the same as syllables, but quite often printed letters are silent, and sometimes you say a sound when there is no letter printed e.g. syllable becomes sil a bul. It is not possible to spell out sounds and syllaphones in ordinary English. This is because, as you are no doubt aware, the English language contains all sorts of inconsistencies—we use only 26 letters to cover about 40 sounds (think of ng in finger, singer and the Aboriginal name Ngunnawal, for example).

The first thing we need to learn is how the sounds and syllaphones work together.

# EXERCISE 12: SYLLAPHONES #2

Read your sentence with the syllaphones equally spaced:

> yaw peh ment will bi pro sest bai i lek tron ik funds trans fer

Did you find it easy to make the pauses between each syllaphone exactly the same length in time? Experiment with this several times until you can do it accurately. Try doing it with longer pauses and shorter pauses. Then try doing it with the syllaphones in different orders: back to front, or mixed up in other ways:

> peh yaw pro ment will bai tron bi sest i trans lek ik funds fer

Of course, you will notice that when you play your readings back, the meaning disappears. However, you might also note that some quite weird effects are achieved, especially when you rearrange the order of the syllaphones. Some 'post-modern' performers turn exercises like these into voice performances. You might also notice that 'rap' or hip-hop is a form of speaking/singing which also works by controlling the pauses between syllaphones.

As you will find when you work through Scene 2: Beats and pauses, being conscious of the sounds and syllaphones and being able to control how you use the pauses, is the key to creating the emotional effects that you want as an actor.

This is because moments of silence are the times when your character appears to be thinking about what's happening or trying to deal with their feelings. Your audience uses the moments of silence to try to work out what the character is thinking and to respond to the feelings. This is the key to acting because it is in these moments that you, the actor, create a relationship with your audience. In the end it is your skill at creating this relationship which makes you a professional actor.

If you are working on the technical and management side, it is necessary for you to understand how important the silences are. You need to be sensitive to what the actors are doing, so you don't accidentally break the silence. On the other hand, if a silence is happening which is beyond the actor's control, then you need to be aware of that so that you can take action to rescue the actor.

An example might help. In *All My Sons* by Arthur Miller, the father gradually comes to realise that he was the cause of his own favourite son's death. His wife and his other son also learn the truth, as do the audience. In the final act, the talk between the characters reaches a point where the truth cannot be avoided any longer. They finally stop talking, and the father, in silence, leaves the stage (the backyard) and walks through the 'back door' in the set into the 'house'. His wife and other son are left on stage. After some time a light turns on which appears to come from an upstairs room, presumably a bedroom. Finally there is a gunshot.

After the shot, the lights fade slowly in silence during which the audience recovers their composure after the shock of the shot. They recognise that the father has committed suicide and have time to reflect on the reasons why this was necessary even as they feel the terror he must have felt as he made his decision. The silence must be maintained for at least a minute, maybe even two minutes, before the lights can be brought up to reveal the actors downstage ready to take their curtain call.

Who controls these silences? As the talk fades, the actors are in control, pausing not only between each speech, but between syllaphones within speeches. As they do this they create a greater and greater sense of tension which must have some kind of resolution. As the father leaves the stage, the control of the silences is taken over by the stage manager and the lighting operator.

If the time between the father's exit and the light appearing is too short, the tension will be relieved too quickly, and the ending will become melodramatic. People in the audience will know too soon that he will commit suicide. If the time is too long, people will become edgy and anxious and start to wonder if that's the end of the play. They might begin to clap before the gunshot, which would ruin the end.

When the light comes on, the audience know that more is to come, but they now do not know what will happen. If the time between the light coming on and the gunshot is too short, the shock of the shot will be lessened because people are still reacting to the light. If the time is too long, they will be left with their thoughts and feelings 'hanging' without resolution and they will begin to lose the strength of the feelings the actors had built up, maybe worrying about whether there will be any resolution.

Each night, the audience is different. The stage manager and lighting operator have to be able to sense the way the audience is reacting. They can't necessarily make the silences the same length each night. The director will have set the times they felt were right in rehearsal, but for each performance the stage manager must run the show to get the right effect.

If the stage manager and lighting operator get it wrong, it's not just the author or the newspaper critic who will be upset. It's not only the audience who will feel cheated, even if they don't quite know why. The actors may well be ropeable. They will feel that all their work in setting up the right level of tension to lead to the horror of the suicide was wasted. And of course, the mother and second son are still visible on stage until the final fade. Their reactions in those long silences add to the audience's feelings and understanding, and the wrong timing will leave them embarrassed on stage. The stage manager and lighting operator are not visible to the audience, so any feelings of blame for a weak ending will flow from the audience to the people they can see: the actors. The right timing makes the curtain call a powerful time of celebration and appreciation. The wrong timing...!

A good actor will also make sure they have experience in technical work, management and directing, so that they have a feel for the technical complications and the special skills which apply backstage. I also encourage people working in front-of-house to have a wide experience. The usher who opens the exit doors too early, or too noisily, during the curtain call can help to break the feeling of celebration between the audience and the actors in a play like *All My Sons*. The houselights will need to come up gently and not too bright at first. Harsher light from the foyer should not be introduced too soon.

A different kind of example is where an actor has

come unstuck. Someone may forget their lines and not be able to improvise. A silence may begin to grow to enormous proportions and become a horrifying black hole. The stage manager should know the play so well that they can recognise the problem very quickly and set something up to fill the gap. It may be necessary to bring in a sound cue which is not supposed to be used till later, or was used earlier. Maybe the lights can be dimmed or brightened. Maybe another actor can be cued in earlier than normal.

In other words, theatre is a total dramatic experience and everyone involved in the production is responsible for supporting what the actors create.

## EXERCISE 13: SYLLAPHONES #3

Really begin to play with your syllaphones:

yaw peh ment will bi pro sest bai i lek tron ik funds trans fer

peh yaw pro ment will bai tron bi sest i trans lek ik funds fer

Say them with many variations of lengths of pausing. Say them monotone. Say them with a different pitch (low note or high note) on each syllaphone. Say them with a different volume (loud or soft) on each syllaphone. Sing your syllaphones in different styles: rap, opera, country and western, crooning ballad, different rock styles.

Really let yourself go. Dance around the room while you sing the syllaphones; do them monotone a la Humphrey Bogart; do them as a child rolling around on the floor (playing happily or in a tantrum); do them as Lady Macbeth in her 'Unsex me here' speech; do them in different accents. Try out all the variations you can imagine.

If you had fun doing this exercise, that's how it should be! Make your own choice of a line from a play, poem or song, and play with your syllaphones.

You should keep coming back to this exercise throughout your training and your career—it will teach you that you are free to express yourself without worrying about the way you sound. The exercise should also help you not to stereotype the way you speak: you do not have to sound impressive when you speak Shakespeare or always speak your broadest Australian/Cockney for lower class characters; funny characters do not always speak Scottish; and nice young ladies do not always speak upper class English.

The basic elements of speech are:
- individual sounds
- syllaphones   (sound groups)
- pauses        (silence between syllaphones)
- pitch         (sound frequency)
- volume        (sound amplitude)

You may not have previously thought of acting as being closely related to physics, yet everyone knows that acting is a physical activity.

When you play a musical instrument, like a guitar, you make sounds by physically moving the strings: these are the notes. You put pauses between sounds, and you change the lengths of the pauses: this is how you create rhythm. The pitch varies depending on where you hold the string against the fret: a short string makes a high pitch note, and a long string makes a low pitch note. The volume of the note depends on how hard you pluck the string: a light touch makes a soft note; if your finger hits the string hard, it makes a loud note.

A great deal of the physics you learned in junior

high school, about wave motion particularly, began with studies (originally by the ancient Greeks) of musical instruments. When you speak you are using parts of your own body just like a musical instrument. The strings are your vocal cords: lengthening and shortening them will change the pitch of your voice, and the speed at which you force air from your lungs past your vocal chords determines the volume. Just as with music, silence in speech is often as effective as sound.

## SCENE 3
## Beats and pauses

Different directors, actors and theatre teachers use different terminology. This is not a bad thing—it shows that people working in theatre change their ideas and don't follow 'the rules'. If they did, theatre would stop being creative.

A beat basically means a change of thought or feeling for the character. Some people use beat only for a major change, such as when a character suddenly realises part way through a speech that things aren't really what they thought they were. They do a kind of 'double take': stop, re-think, and then say or do something quite different from what it seemed they would do.

This happens to Macbeth, for example:

MACBETH: Let fall thy blade on vulnerable crests,
   I bear a charmed life, which must not yield
   To one of woman born.
MACDUFF: Despair thy charm,
   And let the Angel whom thou still hast serv'd
   Tell thee, Macduff was from his mother's womb
   Untimely ripp'd.

MACBETH: Accursed be that tongue that tells me so,
 For it hath cow'd my better part of man:
 … I'll not fight with thee.

There is a beat before Macbeth says 'Accursed be that tongue that tells me so', as indicated by Macduff's short line 'Untimely ripp'd'. What Macduff says stymies Macbeth. His confidence in his power is completely undermined. He realises that he can lose the fight, and his feelings change dramatically. Logically, of course, if he fought with all his old determination, there is no reason why he should not win. But he is a superstitious man, as we have seen many times earlier in the play, so Macduff's news suddenly drains all Macbeth's bravery and, uncharacteristically, he begins to try to negotiate his way out of the fight.

Most characters will have an experience like this, and these moments are a useful tool for analysing the dramatic structure of a play. I usually call these moments 'turning points' or 'shifts in a character's understanding'. I use the word 'beat' for the smaller changes which happen often during a character's speech or action. Analysing the beats in a character's speeches will give you an understanding of some of the more subtle aspects of the character.

In naturalistic drama, each speech or action has beats, each scene has one shift, and there is one turning point in the play. In the ABC's television series *SeaChange,* for example, each group of characters had their own storyline which ran parallel with that of the main character, Laura. Each scene shift concerned only one group of characters. The turning point of the series was the flooding of the tunnel, as at that moment every character experienced a major shift. This turning point completed the dramatic structure of the show, and the series finished soon after.

We will now look at how beats and pauses work in naturalistic and realist drama.

## Naturalism

The late 19th century saw a shift from melodrama to naturalism and realism in drama. For our first exercise we will look at some dialogue from *A Doll's House* by Henrik Ibsen.

## **EXERCISE 14: BEATS AND PAUSES #1**

*A Doll's House*
by Henrik Ibsen
translated by Peter Watts
Penguin 1965

MRS LINDE: So it all had to come out of your own pocket-money? Poor Nora.

NORA: Of course. After all, it was my own doing. So whenever Torvald gave me money for new dresses and things, I never spent more than half of it—I always bought the simplest, cheapest things. Thank goodness anything looks well on me, so Torvald never noticed. But, oh Kristina, it hasn't been at all easy, because it's so nice to be beautifully dressed, isn't it?

MRS LINDE: It certainly is.

NORA: Then I've found other ways of earning money too. Last winter I was lucky enough to get a lot of copying to do, so I locked myself in and sat writing—often till after midnight. Oh, I was so tired sometimes ... so tired. Still, it was really tremendous fun sitting there working and earning money. It was almost like being a man.

MRS LINDE: But how much have you been able to pay off?

NORA: Well, I don't know exactly. You see, with a thing like that, it's very difficult to keep accounts. All I know is that I've paid out every penny that I've been able to scrape together. Often I've been at my wits' end. ... (*Smiling*) Then I used to sit here and imagine that a rich old gentleman had fallen in love with me—

First of all look for the syllaphones and get used to dividing the words into sounds:

MRS LINDE: So | it | all | had | to | come | out | of | your | own | po | cket | -mo | ney? | Poor | Nor | a.

NORA: Of | course. | Af | ter | all, | it | was | my | own | do | ing. | So | when | e | ver | Tor | vald | gave | me | mo | ney | for | new | dre | sses | and | things, | I | ne | ver | spent | more | than | half | of | it | —I | al | ways | bought | the | sim | plest, | chea | pest | things.

You will notice that the words are almost all one or two syllables, and the speech sounds like ordinary conversation. This is an important feature in naturalism.

But in fact Mrs Linde and Nora are in a quite tense relationship at this point of the play. They both have things to hide and to reveal. In order to find the beats, consider the pauses each of the characters make and try to figure out what would be going through her mind as she pauses. For example:

MRS LINDE: So it all (*beat: I wonder how much money was really involved—I bet it wasn't really a worry when you think about her husband being a bank manager*) had to come out of your own (*beat: poor little dear!*) pocket-money? (*beat: She hasn't got a clue about what being poor is really like*) Poor Nora.

NORA: Of course. (*beat: There's something going on here but I can't quite follow her drift*) After all, it was my own doing. So (*beat: I'd better justify myself*) whenever Torvald gave me money for new dresses and things, I never spent more than half of it—(*beat: I know it sounds a bit lame*) I always bought the simplest, cheapest things.

Read the parts aloud, on tape if you wish, with pauses for the beats. Do you think that my suggestions work? Experiment with other ways of finding beats, such as using Stanislavsky's method of 'intention' or 'objective'. For example:

NORA: Of course. (*beat: I won't let her make fun of me*) After all, it was my own doing. So (*beat: I'll show her I'm practical too*) whenever Torvald gave me money for new dresses and things, I never spent more than half of it—(*beat: This'll put her in her place*) I always bought the simplest, cheapest things.

*Coralie Lansdowne Says No*
by Alex Buzo
Currency Press 1974

*Late that night.* STUART *is asleep on the sofa, the book on his chest. Silence.* CORALIE *appears in the right doorway. She stands there very still. She carries her shoes in her hand. When she starts to speak,* STUART *wakes up and looks at her.*

CORALIE: Night makes it better, you know. The whole area seems reasonably beautiful, the whole palsied landscape seems tangible when you're down by the beach looking up and you walk through the shadows of the bananas and there aren't all that many lights. The freaks are asleep. All the moaning has stopped. It's silent, like a ship in the night. I've been down on the beach and among the bananas. I've been there for hours. I left the party, left all the creeps to drink and talk and line up screws for the night. I left my 'escort', he was far too charming, and he frightened me a bit because he really is serious and he does seem to want me for something I can't face at all. So I left and walked and walked and sat on the beach and looked at the outline, the rocks and gums, the cracked shells and clustered droppings with very few lights and freaks within and I surged up inside because I wasn't really part of this design, this conspiracy. And the surging peaked and then sank inside and I lay on the sand and I thought of the party and him and what he wanted me to do and the more I thought and the deeper I got into the night the more blurred the landscape became and the hill seemed like floodlights through a skeleton and the humming got louder so I went for a paddle in the sea. And I tried to think and my thoughts were physically painful and I walked through the rocks and the trees, through the bananas and heard the odd snatch of freaky life as I hauled up the steps to the top, where the most frightening thing of all was that this house seemed almost comforting.

*She is by now sitting on the sofa beside* STUART. *They kiss.*

You'll have to treat me well. I must be treated well.
*Fade out.*

When you break this speech into syllaphones, and you think about volume and pitch, you'll find that it seems almost like a piece of music. Some syllaphones should be stressed more than others, but you must be careful not to make the rhythm too obvious by overemphasising some of the syllaphones. Alternatively, speaking in a monotone (making each syllaphone evenly spaced) will kill the rhythm.

In this speech there is an underlying 4-stress pattern, which is the most common rhythm in the English language.

The whole area seems reasonably beautiful |

the whole palsied landscape seems tangible

There are, however, phrases that have only 3 stresses, and others that have 5.

and my thoughts were physically painful |

and I walked through the rocks and the trees |

where the most frightening thing of all was that this

house seemed almost comforting

There are also some phrases with 2 stresses next to others with 2, or next to others with 3.

I've been there for hours. | I left the party

he does seem to want me | for something I can't

seem to face at all.

In the last example, there is perhaps half a stress on the final word 'all'.

Alex Buzo has played around with the ordinary 4-stress rhythm, like a good musician, so that the rhythm doesn't become too regular and boring. With all speeches you must explore how the beats that you place between words or syllaphones can work with the underlying rhythm and create space for the character's feelings to become apparent.

## EXERCISE 15: BEATS AND PAUSES IN *CORALIE LANSDOWNE SAYS NO*

Mark out all the stresses in Coralie's speech. Put in the 'bar' marks. Choose a section of about four lines (for example 'The whole area seems reasonably beautiful ... aren't all that many lights') and mark in all the places where you could put beats. Then read the section onto tape four times, using different variations of beats. Play back the tape and see which versions seem more real, and which seem more melodramatic. Try to find a reading which is both real and dramatically powerful.

What did you find? Did it take you a long time to do the job thoroughly? Did you know what Coralie was thinking at each beat? You may have decided that she would hesitate on the word 'conspiracy':

this con | spiracy

There are many possibilities as to why she would do this. She may think:

- I'm getting too negative about all this.
- I've started to say it now. Stuart will think I'm a wimp if I don't say what I really think.
- This'll be a test for Stuart. Does he see all this the same way as me?

How do you know which is right? The answer is that any of them may be right, and there are many other possibilities.

# EXERCISE 16: BEATS AND PAUSES IN *FURTIVE LOVE*

Mark out all the stresses in the speech below. Put in the 'bar' marks. Choose a section of about four lines (for example 'And that was it needed … believed I'd let him down') and mark in all the places where you could put beats. Then read the section onto tape four times, using different variations of beats, including breaking the pattern of the full stops. Play back the tape and see which versions seem more real, and which seem more melodramatic. Try to find a reading which is both real and dramatically powerful.

*Furtive Love*
by Peter Kenna
Currency Press, 1980

TOM: You're so hard on yourself. I first made love to another man the night before my wedding. Some of the chaps I worked with gave me a stag party. One of them had often made it clear he was fond of me but I'd never taken him seriously. I was in love with the girl I was going to marry. There was, of course, a lot of drink at the party but that wasn't what made this man seem suddenly attractive. For some reason—perhaps it had been inside me all the time and I wasn't aware of it—I dared to consider that another man might be attractive. And that was all it needed. I went home to his place, stayed the night with him and the next morning I got married. I discovered I was in love with two people who each satisfied a different need in me. But the man believed I'd let him down. After a while we began to quarrel. We'd make it up, but it would always break out again: his distress at the situation. Eventually he killed himself. And I thought I would die too—of grief and guilt. So I turned to the other person I loved. I told my wife everything. If I'd been sane enough to stop and think about it I might have realised she'd be appalled. But I wasn't. And she's never permitted me to make love to her since. Never even touched me with a gesture of concern. We have an arrangement because of the children. She won't divorce me if I behave discreetly. I don't want a divorce. I still love her. I'm not a fool, Joe. I suspect you all regard my caution as a joke. I'm aware I've probably become a rather boring person. But outside my bedroom, I'm never sure of how I ought to behave. And I walk in dread of another calamity.

Finding the beats and pauses in a speech is fine and detailed work. Each pause will emphasise the word or phrase which comes next, giving it a special significance. The character has just stopped and thought or felt something different, and the audience picks up the change and 'hears' the personal meaning that the character gives the speech.

We do this all the time when we are talking in real life. You'll know from your own experience that someone talking without pausing is probably not listening to you, and perhaps not listening to themselves. They may be very excited about something, or covering up their feelings.

Short pauses often indicate that the speaker is thinking and is aware of having an effect on someone else. They can make what they say funny or mildly dramatic with pauses from about one to three seconds. When pauses get much longer, the effect is likely to be much more serious, and increase the listener's empathy with the speaker.

## EXERCISE 17: MOTHER, I'M HOME

Experiment with pauses of different lengths, from almost none through to some up to three, ten and then thirty seconds, speaking the famous line: Mother, I'm home.

Take note of the different meanings and feelings which you are able to create with different length pauses placed at each of the possible beats:

Mo | ther, | I'm | home.

For extreme effects, you can even place short pauses in

I' | m and ho| me.

Choose lines from a script and experiment with them, exploring what happens if you make all the pauses the same length, or if you vary the length of pauses. You should find the strength of the point (the special meaning of the following word) is greater when a pause is longer in comparison with the pauses around it, and is weaker if all the pauses are the same length. Regular long pauses will kill the emotional quality stone dead (and may make the audience think you've lost your lines).

Once you have the idea of looking for beats and especially remembering that they come in the pauses (and that these can come in the middle of words sometimes, and don't always relate to standard punctuation marks), you are ready to move on to the next step: through-lines.

## SCENE 4
## Through-lines

As with beats, you'll find people use the term through-line in different ways, so if you find my method a bit different, don't worry. My approach doesn't conflict with other approaches—it's a useful addition.

## Whole play through-line

The most common idea is about the through-line of a play. This is sometimes called the spine. It is the job of the director to find a line of development that runs from the beginning of the play to the end of the play that the audience can follow. If there isn't a through-line the audience will feel that the production is uncoordinated (which means they will lose interest) and they won't understand what the play is about.

Unfortunately, it's often in amateur Shakespeare productions that finding a through-line gets forgotten. Take *Macbeth*. By the time you're involved in doing witches' cauldrons, mad scenes and fight scenes, you can end up with a play which is a series of exciting bits with boring bits in between. Of course, that's not what Shakespeare wanted—nor what your audience wants.

A good director will decide what line they want to project through *Macbeth*. Is it the diary of a weak man who wants power but can't take the pace? (This could be set in a New York company boardroom.) Is it about a woman who wants to be a man? (Lady Macbeth might reappear at the end in this production to remind us of her role and reflect on how she failed. Maybe this is a production criticising extreme feminist attitudes.) Or maybe it's a play about violence and its effects on people. (In which case each scene is designed to build horror on horror—but the question will be, does this encourage violence in the audience or turn them off violence? The director's through-line should be clear on this point.)

When you present an audition piece, you face the problem that you are doing the speech in isolation, not as part of a production. Because you haven't got a director to give you a through-line, you're going to have to work something out for yourself. Study the play which your speech came from to find a through-line.

## Character through-line

Like the whole play through-line, each character needs a through-line for their part in the play. The last line of Chekhov's *The Seagull*, spoken by Dorn privately to Trigorin so the others can't hear, is 'The fact is, Konstantin Gavrilovich has shot himself…'

The actor playing Konstantin Gavrilovich Trepliov needs to know the stages of feelings he has at each point in the play which will be shown to the audience so that they can understand why he shot himself. The actor's through-line for the part needs to be consistent with the director's through-line for the whole play so that, for example, the audience feels sympathetic to Trepliov's inability to keep living in a society, in which he feels is a complete failure, or maybe the audience feels that Trepliov is the failure and his death is his own fault because he took no action to change his society.

It's important that questions about the whole play's through-line and each character's through-line are resolved during the rehearsal process. Some directors have all the answers early on, sometimes even before the actors are cast. Some reach the answers in the first days of rehearsal, through readings and discussions. Some find the answers quite late as they and the actors work together. Each approach is as good as the other, so long as everyone is clear about what they are doing when they get on stage in front of the paying audience.

## Single speech through-line

In your audition you will have to present a single speech without its context, and so you have to do much more preparation than you might for a single speech when it's part of a production. However, the technique I will give you in this section can often be useful in rehearsal for a play when a particular speech becomes a block for you. Maybe it never seems to come out quite right, or maybe you can't seem to get it quite how the director wants it. Doing an emotional graph may help you find the solution.

The through-line can be drawn like a graph which shows the emotional intensity at each point in the speech. For an effective speech there are usually two or more through-lines going at once. For your first audition, working on two through-lines will probably be as much as you want (or need) to attempt. However, once you know the technique of graphing emotions, you can extend the method and graph as many through-lines as you (or the director) feel you require.

## EXERCISE 18: RESPONSE TO SELF

Choose a modern naturalistic speech, such as Coralie or Tom above. Do the basic work on syllaphones, beats and pauses so that you have a feel for the language. Present the speech in different ways, and in different accents.

When you can present the speech in different ways and have a feel for the language, write down the answers to these questions:

1. What does the character feel about him/herself at the beginning of the speech?

2. What does the character feel about him/herself at the end of the speech?

Try to avoid words which describe what the character thinks; instead, find words that describe how they feel.

Next, repeat the exercise using the following speech from *After the Fall* by Arthur Miller. (Viking Press 1968), and then graph Mother's response to herself.

MOTHER: To this day he walks into a room you want to bow! *Warmly*. Any restaurant—one look at him and the waiters start moving tables around. *Because*, dear, people know that this is a *man*. Even Doctor Strauss, at my wedding he came over to me, says, 'Rose, I can see it looking at him, you've got a wonderful man,' and he was always in love with me, Strauss. ... Oh, sure, but he was only a penniless medical student then, my father wouldn't let him in the house. Who knew he'd end up so big in the gallstones? That poor boy! Used to bring me novels to read, poetry, philosophy, God knows what! One time we even sneaked off to hear Rachmaninoff together. *She laughs sadly; and with wonder more than bitterness*. That's why, you see, two weeks after we were married; sit down to dinner and Papa hands me a menu and asks me to read it to him. Couldn't *read*! I got so frightened I nearly ran away! ... Why? Because your grandmother is such a fine, unselfish woman; two months in school and they put him into the shop! That's what some women are, my dear— and now he goes and buys her a new Packard every year. *With a strange and deep fear*. Please, darling, I want you to *draw* the letters, that scribbling is ugly, dear; and your posture, your speech, it can all be beautiful! Ask Miss Fisher, for years they kept my handwriting pinned up on the bulletin board; God, I'll never forget it, valedictorian of the class with a scholarship to Hunter in my hand ... *A blackness flows into her soul*. And I came home, and Grandpa says, 'You're getting married!' I was like—like with small wings, just getting ready to fly; I slept all year with the catalogue under my pillow. To learn, to learn everything! Oh, darling, the whole thing is such a mystery!

You may decide that Mother feels self-confident and self-important at the beginning of the speech (she is evidently proud of her husband's prowess), yet at the end she feels entirely lacking in self-esteem.

To graph the emotions, you will need to draw a line from 'self-importance' to 'no confidence', but you also need to decide on the level of intensity of each of these feelings, so you may end up with a graph which looks like this:

### *AFTER THE FALL* BY ARTHUR MILLER

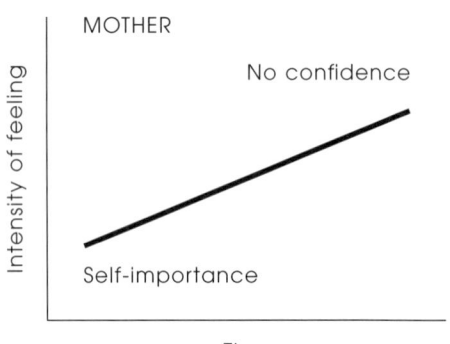

MOTHER

*[Graph: Intensity of feeling vs Time, showing a line rising from 'Self-importance' at lower left to 'No confidence' at upper right]*

The graph tells you that emotional intensity is not the same as positive or negative emotion. Although Mother feels self-important at the beginning, the feeling isn't intense as it is a reflection of her feelings towards her husband rather than herself. By the end she has lost the sense of self-importance to the point of having no confidence in herself, and this insecurity is quite intense, as Miller demonstrates in the direction 'A blackness flows into her soul'.

Try reading your speech (don't do it from memory at this stage) with the feelings you decide the character has about him/herself at the beginning and the end. Coralie Lansdowne, for example, may begin the speech feeling quite unsure of herself, but ends the speech thoroughly in control. Tom feels outwardly in control at the beginning, but this is an act: underneath he is aware of his insecurity. By the end his sense of his own weakness has strengthened, though he covers this by even better acting. The graphs may look like this:

*CORALIE LANSDOWNE SAYS NO* BY ALEX BUZO

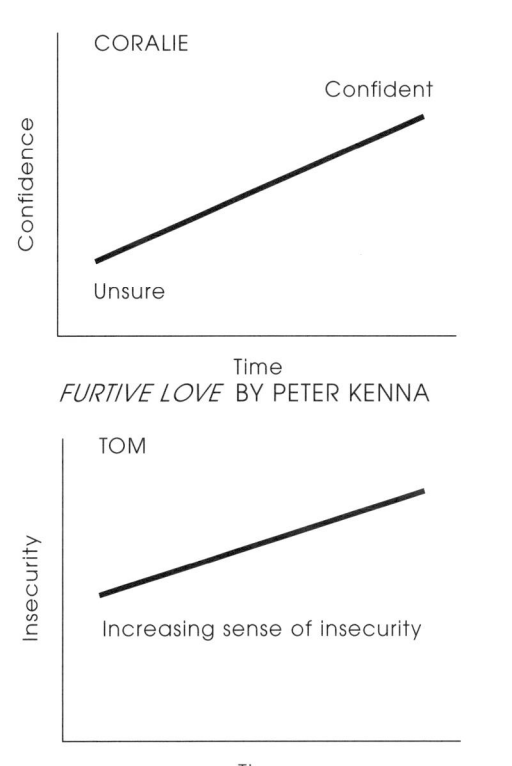

*FURTIVE LOVE* BY PETER KENNA

In my readings, Coralie's strength of feeling about herself rises markedly during her speech as she changes from the negative to the positive, but Tom's strength of feeling doesn't seem to change much on the surface; but deeper down his insecurity has increased considerably. So the through-line in response to self has two components: the feeling and the strength of feeling

You may also have noticed that at some point in the speech, the character's feeling may have made a definite change. In Mother's speech, for example, Miller helps by putting in stage directions 'With a strange and deep fear' but you should remember that this script is the final version after production, and Miller has recorded what the actor found in the lines in performance. You might find a change at a different point, according to the feelings you are working with.

In Mother's speech Miller indicates two points of change, and this shows you that the line from the beginning feeling to the end feeling may not be straight. The intensity level might be flat for a while and then quite suddenly go up or down. By experimenting with your speech and character you can draw your own graph.

Don't be too hard on yourself at this point about whether you have got it 'right' or not. Just as directors have to 'find' the through-line for the play which suits them, so you are looking for a line that works for you.

You may have noticed when you were doing Exercise 18 that the through-line seemed a little simplistic, as in reality people experience more than one emotion at a time. For example, in Mother's speech, you can see that she has varying emotions about her husband, as well as Doctor Strauss and her son. Coralie discovers that her feelings towards Stuart are not what she originally thought them to be. Tom's feelings about Joe appear to grow as if he is gaining confidence, even as his underlying insecurity is increasing: it's not easy to know how honest he is being with his self and with Joe—he may be attempting to manipulate Joe into having sex.

## EXERCISE 19: RESPONSE TO THE OTHER
In this exercise you ask two more questions:
1. What does the character feel about the other at the beginning of the speech?
2. What does the character feel about the other at the end of the speech?

Remembering to avoid what the character thinks, concentrating instead on what they feel.

But what do I mean by the other?

Depending on the character and the play they are in, the other could be either a person, an object, a situation, or an idea.

For example, when Macbeth hears Macduff's threat that he can't be killed because he was not 'born of woman', Macbeth's 'the other' is no longer Macduff, the ordinary man he can certainly defeat—it is his belief in what the witches had told him. He now believes, with a frightening intensity, that he will not be able to defeat Macduff, and he tries to beg off the fight. This intensity remains with Macbeth through to his death.

In Mother's speech from *After the Fall*, it makes sense to take her husband as the other, although it is not her husband as he is at the present time, but more as she thought he was in the past. Or perhaps at the beginning of the speech the other is in the past but by the end he is in the present.

For Coralie, Stuart is the obvious 'other', but he might

represent something more for her—perhaps the idea of a permanent partner.

For Tom, the immediate 'other' is Joe, but you might consider playing Tom with two 'others': how he feels heterosexual society sees him as a married man, precariously balanced against how homosexual society sees him.

As you can see, working out the character's response to the other brings a great deal of complexity to the through-lines. By working on the character's response to the other you should be able to find the sub-text of the speech—the meaning for the character that they are not able to directly express. It is the sub-text of a play which makes the audience respond to the drama. As you use your beats, pauses and through-lines, you create a character which the audience has to 'read', as if the character were a real person.

I'll suggest that in Mother's speech, she begins feeling a sense of awe towards the other and by the end she has become afraid of the other. The intensity of feeling at the start is very high—and so is the intensity of feeling at the end. So her emotional graph might look like this:

### *AFTER THE FALL* BY ARTHUR MILLER

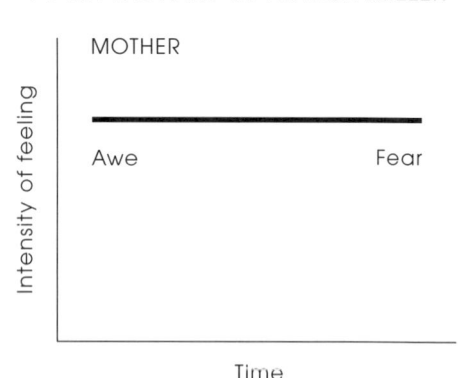

**MOTHER**

*(Graph: Intensity of feeling vs Time; a horizontal line at high intensity from "Awe" to "Fear")*

In Coralie's case, she may begin by feeling threatened by Stuart's presence when she first sees him, but by the end of the speech she has accepted and even welcomes his presence.

In Tom's speech, taking Joe (and the homosexual society's acceptance of Tom) as the other, Tom may begin the speech feeling very determined to get his way and by the end his manner may be almost aggressive as he sees he has won Joe over.

Try doing your own graph that charts your character's response to the other. Then do a reading in which you focus on this emotional through-line. (It's still best to read rather than try to work from memory, and use pencil so you are able to make changes easily.)

As with your first through-line you may notice that there is a shift point where the feeling changes (gets stronger; or weaker; or changes direction), or there may be more than one shift.

Mark your beats, lengths of pauses, notes about feelings at beginning and end, and the shift points you have found in your through-lines.

You may be feeling a bit daunted by the amount of work you need to do on just one speech. I can, however, promise you that, like the work on syllaphones, pauses and beats, once you practise this technique for finding through-lines, you will learn to do it naturally. If you're like me, you may even picture your first graph as you do your first reading of the speech, get the feel of the other quite quickly on the second reading, and sense the shift points as this happens. This will mean that you are able to do a competent reading almost immediately.

# **EXERCISE 20: RESPONSE TO SELF AND THE OTHER**

It is now time to put your two graphs together, so you are able to see both the character's response to self, and to the other. With my reading of Mother, the graph looks like this:

### *AFTER THE FALL* BY ARTHUR MILLER

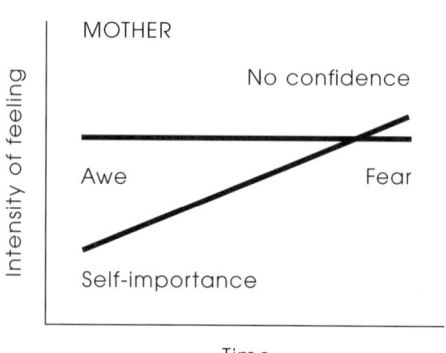

MOTHER

Intensity of feeling / Time

No confidence

Awe — Fear

Self-importance

Try out your own double through-line graph.

You will usually find that the intensity lines come close together or cross at some point, often near (but not at) the end of the speech. This joining or crossing point is the most intense shift point in the speech and there will often be a substantial beat at this point. For example, in Tom's speech, Kenna has made the main shift point clear: 'I still love her. (*Beat*) I'm not a fool, Joe.' Try reading your speech with both through-lines going at once and see if you can establish the full strength of feeling at the shift point.

The shift point in your speech may not be the shift for the whole scene—although quite often a good audition piece is the speech which contains the scene's shift. When you are doing an audition, the speech becomes like a very short play in its own right. It only lasts about two minutes, but if you are going to have a real impact on your audience—the auditioners—the shift point in the speech has to be equivalent to the turning point of a play.

If you are working on a speech and are not able to find a strong shift point it may be for a number of reasons. It may be that the script is poorly written, or it may simply not be an appropriate audition piece. Another possibility is that it is not naturalistic—these exercises are written for naturalistic plays.

It's good to have an aim for your professional career. Successfully creating one through-line is a major achievement; making two through-lines work creates a complex character that most people in the audience will feel is real. Great actors are often able to achieve three or more through-lines, in which case the audience forgets they are watching an actor and become totally engaged in identifying with the character.

The actor should be totally engaged in creating the character. Always aim to reach the point where skill (technique) and craft (sensitivity) become art.

At this point I'll mention the business of learning lines. As you prepare for an audition, you don't need to learn the lines until you have done all the technical work. In fact by the time you have studied the syllaphones, the beats and pauses, and the through-lines, you'll probably just about be able to work from memory.

In a production process, you may be expected to come to rehearsal with your lines already memorised. If so, learn the lines in neutral—that is without committing yourself to particular beats and through-lines. As the director works with you, the techniques you have learned will come into play and the character will form.

## SCENE 5
## Shakespeare, Shaw and Brecht

These three playwrights have had the greatest influence on non-naturalistic plays. In Australia, we have developed our own styles of theatre, especially since the days of La Mama in Melbourne and Nimrod in Sydney in the 1960s and 1970s. We now have a great many playwrights whose plays are non-naturalistic, but understanding the techniques for working with William Shakespeare, George Bernard Shaw and Bertolt Brecht will give you the range you need to take up training and reach the standards which are expected of professional actors.

It is important for you to research and understand the history of theatre and the writers who influenced it. For example, if you were using a speech by David Williamson you would be expected to learn about the stylistic changes in his writing since the premiere of his first play in the late 1960s. *The Removalists* (1971) may be categorised as naturalistic, but many of his plays written in the 1970s and 1980s tend more towards farce than naturalism with their reliance on one-liners and their carefully constructed plots. Williamson returned to naturalism in the late 1990s with the Jack Manning community conferencing plays, and such works as *Brilliant Lies* and *Heretic*. Knowledge of the New Wave of Australian theatre of the 1960s and the subsequent changes in Williamson's style of writing will help you decide what approach you should take when preparing your audition speech.

## William Shakespeare

There are many similarities between Shakespeare's and the modern world, but the biggest difference is perhaps that England in the 17th century was much more dangerous than Australia is in the early 21st century. From an acting point of view, popular music since the Beatles may be the key to understanding Shakespeare. In his time people in pubs sang complicated music quite naturally. Madrigals of the time could have four, five, or even more parts. In modern songs there are not often so many separate voice parts all going at once, but the syncopation, off-beat timing and unusual ways of patterning stresses creates quite similar effects to the most complex Elizabethan music.

This book isn't going to become a study of music (you should do that for yourself) but music is the beginning point for analysing Shakespeare's language. Shakespeare was a poet living in a musical culture, and hopefully you are too.

In order to analyse a speech from Shakespeare, you will need to discover the naturalistic emotional through-lines, use Stanlislavsky's method to follow the character's objectives, and do an extended study of syllaphones, pauses, beats and rhythms. (You will notice that sometimes I use 'beat' in the musical sense to mean the regular stressed sounds which create the rhythm.)

One speech I shall use is from *The Winter's Tale*, when Queen Hermione, imprisoned by her husband Leontes, demands that the truth (the oracle of Apollo) be heard. Her wish is granted, and the oracle clearly removes all suspicion from her. Leontes refuses to believe the oracle—and thus the bringing of this proud king to his knees is set in train.

I'll also give an example from *Henry IV*, when Hotspur defends his actions.

*Complete works of William Shakespeare*
Murrays, nd.

HERMIONE: Sir, spare your threats:
    The bug which you would fright me with I seek.
    To me can life be no commodity:
    The crown and comfort of my life, your favour,
    I do give lost; for I do feel it gone,
    But know not how it went. My second joy,
    And first-fruits of my body, from his presence
    I am barr'd, like one infectious. My third comfort,
    Starr'd most unluckily, is from my breast,
    The innocent milk in it most innocent mouth,
    Haled out to murder: myself on every post
    Proclaim'd a strumpet: with immodest hatred
    The child-bed privilege denied, which 'longs
    To women of all fashion: lastly, hurried
    Here to this place, i' the open air, before
    I have got strength of limit. Now, my liege,
    Tell me what blessings I have here alive,
    That I should fear to die? Therefore proceed.
    But yet, hear this; mistake me not; no life,
    I prize it not a straw, but for mine honour,
    Which I would free, if I shall be condemn'd
    Upon surmises, all proofs sleeping else
    But what your jealousies awake, I tell you
    'Tis rigour and not law. Your honours all,
    I do refer me to the oracle:
    Apollo be my judge!

HOTSPUR: My liege, I did deny no prisoners:
But I remember, when the fight was done,
When I was dry with rage and extreme toil,
Breathless and faint, leaning upon my sword,
Came there a certain lord, neat, and trimly dress'd,
Fresh as a bridegroom; and his chin, new reap'd,
Show'd like a stubble-land at harvest home:
He was perfumed like a milliner,
And 'twixt his finger and his thumb he held
A pouncet-box, which ever and anon
He gave his nose and took't away again;
Who therewith angry, when it next came there,
Took it in snuff: and still he smiled and talk'd;
And as the soldiers bore dead bodies by,
He call'd them untaught knaves, unmannerly,
To bring a slovenly unhandsome corpse
Betwixt the wind and his nobility.
With many holiday and lade terms
He question'd me; among the rest, demanded
My prisoners in your majesty's behalf.
I then, all smarting with my wounds being cold,
To be so pester'd with a popinjay,
Out of my grief and my impatience
Answered neglectingly, I know not what,
He should, or he should not; for he made me mad
To see him shine so brisk, and smell so sweet,
And talk so like a waiting-gentlewoman
Of guns, and drums, and wounds, God save the mark!
And telling me the sovereign'st thing on earth
Was parmaceti for an inward bruise;
And that it was great pity, so it was,
That villanous saltpetre should be digg'd
Out of the bowels of the harmless earth,

> Which many a good tall fellow had destroy'd
> So cowardly; and but for these vile guns
> He would himself have been a soldier.
> This bald unjointed chat of his, my lord,
> I answer'd indirectly, as I said;
> And I beseech you, let not his report
> Come current for an accusation
> Betwixt my love and your high majesty.

The publisher of this edition noted 'In this text the plays are presented as they appear in the First Folio of 1623. There is no new reading of the text and only those variations have been included which are agreed by the best Shakespearean critics. For the most part it is Delius's text that is followed'.

This means that you can trust that the words in the speech are original, but the punctuation may not be a reliable interpretation. In Hermione's speech, for example, 'in it mouth' sounds a bit odd when we would say 'in its mouth', but it's possible that Shakespeare may have said (as it still is said in parts of Northern England today) 'in t'mouth'.

Now your attention is focussed on the detail of the language, you should do the usual first step.

## EXERCISE 21: SYLLAPHONES IN SHAKESPEARE

Mark the syllaphones in each speech. Despite the fact that the script was written 400 years ago, this should be a relatively simple exercise.

To | me | can | life | be | no | com | mod | i | ty

Before you begin to look for beats and pauses, as you would do in modern naturalistic script, the next step is to learn some technical things about Shakespeare's language. Although he sometimes used prose (that is, ordinary English in 4 beat rhythm as used by Buzo in *Coralie Lansdowne Says No*), this was mainly for comic contrast to the serious drama of his plays, or to contrast lower and upper class characters. Good examples are the Porter's speech in *Macbeth*, and the workmen in *A Midsummer Night's Dream*.

Most of the time Shakespeare wrote in a special kind of verse. In his time, educated people were fascinated by books that had been written in the past, particularly old Roman books. Latin was a well known language in Shakespeare's Europe, being the language of the Church of Rome and the language used for writing important books.

Ancient Roman poets, such as Virgil and Ovid, were governed by formal rules relating to their use of syllables and the varying patterns of stresses used when writing on different topics. There isn't any need for you to learn much about these unless you want to, but the story of why Shakespeare wrote 5 beat lines is interesting.

For over 200 years, Geoffrey Chaucer had been England's most celebrated poet. Chaucer wrote using a 4 beat structure (the rhyme royal) which gave the English language a strength and power that was much-needed by the national psyche, as they were fighting the French in the One Hundred Years War at the time.

In Shakespeare's youth, Sir Edmund Spenser went to Italy where he studied Italian poetry, paying particular attention to that of Plutarch. He then returned to England and wrote *The Fairie Queene*, a long poem which both sang the praises of Queen

Elizabeth and demonstrated his own cleverness in using a 'new' 5 beat structure. (Courting the favour of the Queen was a wise move given that the monarchs of the time were not averse to chopping off people's heads.) He also brought back to England a special interest in the Italian sonnet.

Shakespeare, whose own neck was always of concern, saw what was going on, and wrote his plays in the new 5 beat line structure. You'll remember, too, that Shakespeare is famous for some 154 sonnets.

Your next task is to learn about the pentameter—the five beat (penta-meter) line structure that Shakespeare used.

Hermione's speech begins: 'Sir, spare your threats'. This is a short line, as the last line spoken by Leontes is 'Look for no less than death' and Hermione must therefore make up the remaining stresses in her speech. The stress pattern here is:

Look for no less than death.

Sir, spare your threats:

The bug which you would fright me with I seek.

Hotspur begins:

My liege, I did deny no prisoners:

You can see that Shakespeare is using an underlying 5 beat structure, but (unlike the strict ancient Romans) he plays around the beat. So you can decide whether Hermione's 'Sir' really has a full stress, or whether to downgrade 'Sir' a bit. And it's interesting that 'you' in 'which you would' would be stressed in normal

English prose, but here the stress is weaker due to the placement of the word in the overall rhythm pattern. Over her two lines, split between two speakers, there are 10 stresses, but there's room to move.

Hotspur, you can see, has a definite 5-beat line, but the stresses fall to give special emphasis to his message, with 3 stresses in a row on 'de...*ny no pris*...oners'.

Shakespeare's language is musical. If you try singing these lines, you'll find they work well if you syncopate the timing—but it will sound much more like jazz than rap. In fact I came to understand how Shakespeare worked through jazz, and in particular Dave Brubeck's *Take Five*, written in 5/4 time. I also find Indian ragas useful, as they use many different combinations of time from 2 beat to 16 beat (including one piece I remember in 13/7 time!).

## EXERCISE 22: THE PENTAMETER

Using Hermione's or Hotspur's speech, or any other Shakespeare speech which you may plan to use for an audition, mark out the stressed syllables. Then read the speech (maybe in short sections at first) in two ways:

1. Overemphasise the stressed syllables to make the rhythm as obvious as possible (this will not sound very good or make the meaning clear, but will train your brain to sense the rhythm).
2. Read as smoothly as you can, allowing the rhythm to be felt under the surface of the lines rather than being too obvious.

Hopefully you will have found that the lines seem to make sense in the second reading (even if you are not familiar with some of the 400 year old words).

An anecdote which may help: One of my students (who went on to become a professional actor) had a broad Australian accent, but tended to read Shakespeare in a stilted upper class English. The result was incomprehensible. I pointed out that the modern Queen's style of speaking did not exist in the first Queen Elizabeth's day. Shakespeare's accent would have sounded more like a broad country accent—not much different in fact from this student's Tasmanian style. As soon as he read Hotspur in his natural Australian, he found the rhythm and meaning—and a great sense of relief!

You may have noticed something else in the line structure. Nearly every line has a pause built in, usually after either the second or third stress.

Haled out to murder: | myself on every post

This cut in the line is called a caesura. The ancient Latin poets had strict rules about where it came according to the types of stress patterns in the line. Shakespeare mostly wrote iambic pentameter in which you get:

unstress (x) stress (/), unstress stress, unstress stress.

In the line above you can see this in

myself on every post

but you also see that he didn't use this pattern in the first part of the line

Haled out to murder:

In Latin poetry, you were expected to keep to the same kind of 'feet' (like a 'bar' as in music) in each line, but Shakespeare has used three different kinds in this line:

$$/ \text{ x } | \text{ x}/\text{x } | \text{ x}/ \text{ } | \text{ x}/ \text{ } | \text{ x}/$$

English has a natural 4-beat rhythm. By using 5 beats, Shakespeare heightened the poetic impact of his work, and gave his writing greater flexibility.

## EXERCISE 23: THE CAESURA

Using the Hermione speech, or any other Shakespeare speech you may want to use for an audition, mark out the caesura in each line. (Hotspur's caesuras are often ignored, which serves to emphasise his youthful excitement.)

Look for the unusual lines, where Shakespeare plays against the rules like putting a caesura after the first 'foot' or just before the last 'foot' or where he uses two caesuras in a line, for example:

But yet hear this; mistake me not; no life

Consider what dramatic effect Shakespeare gets by playing around with the stresses and caesuras, and you'll appreciate his amazing skill as a writer. Remember, though, that you can place a beat wherever you need—not just at the caesura, and certainly not necessarily at the end of a line. Shakespeare gives you a musical base and the freedom to improvise. This is one of the reasons his work has remained an essential part of theatre for so long.

Apart from Shakespeare, poetic drama is not a common form today. However, once you have become used to looking for the poetic structure in Shakespeare's plays, you will find it easier to prepare for more modern plays written in verse, such as Douglas Stewart's *Fire on the Snow* or T. S. Eliot's *Murder in the Cathedral*. Some modern writers, for example Louis Nowra or Alma de Groen, may use poetic language, although they don't use traditional poetic forms.

Shakespeare's characters are not naturalistic in the modern sense, but they do have motivations and feelings and so you can apply the emotional through-line technique.

## EXERCISE 24: EMOTIONAL THROUGH-LINES IN SHAKESPEARE

Take the Shakespeare speech you plan to use for an audition and prepare your two through-lines: What does the character feel about him/herself? What does the character feel about the other?

For example, Hermione may begin feeling hopeless at a mid level of intensity at the beginning and strong at a high level of intensity at the end; while towards Leontes (her other) she may feel anger at a high level of intensity at the beginning and power at a high level of intensity at the end.

Hotspur may begin feeling self-righteous at a high level of intensity but humble at a high level of intensity at the end; while he may feel afraid of King Henry (his other) at a quite high level of intensity as he begins, ending by feeling confident of the King's acceptance at a fairly high level of intensity.

The other aspect to Shakespeare's writing that you need to remember when you are preparing an audition piece is that his characters constantly re-evaluate how they stand in relation to the other power players. This is true in his comedies as much as his tragedies.

The method developed by Konstantin Stanislavsky

is useful when analysing a speech and understanding the character's motivation. He tried to teach his actors in the early part of the 20th century—when naturalistic plays were still new compared with melodrama—how to break out of over-acting. To be able to act as if they were the character and to appear natural, he explained that the character would have an objective (or intention) each time they speak or move (or remain silent or still).

In Shakespeare's plays, a character's objectives are often to manoeuvre another character into a weaker position. You can think of an objective for a whole speech, but you will often find that a character's objectives will change during a speech, according to the way the character thinks they are succeeding or failing to achieve their objectives.

When you have just a script without author's stage directions, you have to work out from the speeches before and after the one you are working on what you think your character's objective will be as they start the speech and what reaction other characters may be having during the speech.

For example, in Hermione's previous speech she had tried to offer herself sexually to Leontes: 'My life stands in the level of your dreams, / Which I'll lay down'. He rejected her offer and was determined to see her as a criminal—in other words he wanted to enforce his power over her to the point of threatening to kill her.

Hermione then began 'Sir, spare your threats' with a determination to match his strength. As she speaks, she realises that she is getting nowhere with Leontes, so she switches her attention to the surrounding Lords.

In the lines 'is from my breast / The innocent milk' she hopes to play on the natural feelings of the Lords to gain their sympathy (which will place Leontes in a weak position if he keeps insisting on treating her as a criminal). She succeeds with the Lords, but realises she needs a strong backup position which will force Leontes' hand. So she works on the Lords again, making the persuasive legal distinction between 'rigour' and the 'law' which places them in a position where they must accept her demand for the oracle to be presented.

In the following scene, the First Lord reacts as Hermione hoped, and she pushes the point until the oracle is brought in, read, and accepted by the Lords.

By this time, Leontes has been pushed too far. He takes back the power position he seems to have lost by simply refusing to accept that the oracle is true.

## EXERCISE 25: OBJECTIVES ANALYSIS IN SHAKESPEARE

Analyse the objectives of the characters in the Shakespeare speech that you are preparing for audition.

There is a big difference between using emotional through-lines and Stanislavsky's objectives method. Some directors of Shakespeare will make his plays naturalistic for modern audiences, while others emphasise the intellectual game-playing aspect of his plays.

It's ironic that though Stanislavsky's method was designed to help actors play natural characters, it also works for characters who, in Shakespeare's plays, symbolise important themes through their struggle to achieve objectives. This is how Stanislavsky and Shakespeare come together. In many modern plays, Stanislavsky's method of objectives analysis will often be as useful as emotional through-lines. It's a particularly useful method to use when filming shows since film work rarely gives the actor the chance to develop whole through-lines for a part when shots are short and often not taken in sequence.

Stanislavsky was not limited to the objectives method (see *The Actor Prepares*), but also taught emotional techniques. These techniques are made easy to understand in *Acting and Performing* by Hayes Gordon, and are the original source for the emotional through-lines technique I've given you.

The rhythm and music of Shakespeare's language allows the audience to identify with his characters on a personal level (I always feel horrified at Hermione's plight), while at the same time making a social and political comment which is still relevant today (Leontes represents the megalomaniacs who are still to be found, unfortunately, on the political stage). Shakespeare teaches us to both understand ourselves and to seek justice in the world. No wonder his plays still dominate theatre around the world.

## George Bernard Shaw

Shaw began writing plays in the early 1890s. His last play was written around 1950 when he was over 90 years old. His plays were famous, and included *Pygmalion* which was adapted to the popular musical *My Fair Lady*.

The new naturalistic plays from Russia (Chekhov) and Norway (Ibsen) took a while to be translated into English, so they hadn't made much impact on the usual melodramas. Shaw was influenced by Ibsen, but he wanted to change the English people's sentimental view of life. As a socialist, he wanted to expose social problems. His novels were melodramatic and unrealistic, yet he had an ear for language and a sense of humour. His plays became a new form of theatre: comedy which is serious social criticism.

Like Shakespeare's comedies, Shaw's plays are not just humorous but have themes about important issues. The differences stem from the different societies in which they lived: the political system of the early 20th century encouraged open argument on social issues, whereas in Shakespeare's time such comments could be construed as a power play, resulting in violent revenge.

Emotional drama was quite sentimental in the 19th century. Shaw wanted to draw people's attention to important issues, which he attempted by breaking people out of their usual emotional responses. He wrote serious comedies, exaggerating the methods used in melodrama. He structured his characters' speeches to make people laugh, but uncomfortably, or to shift the focus of the audience to the bigger picture rather than the immediate situation. For example, in the speech we will be using from *St Joan*, the emphasis is placed upon the strength of Joan's convictions and beliefs, rather than a melodramatic sadness at her impending death.

Shaw knew, of course, that his ideas would be disturbing or threatening, and he often used comedy to make them more accessible. His first play, *Mrs Warren's Profession*, is about a woman who became wealthy by running a brothel. She paid for her daughter to become a successful lawyer, but without her daughter knowing the source of her money. So there is both comedy in the dilemma of whether her daughter should be told (remembering that in Shaw's day running a brothel was an illegal activity) and social criticism of the illegality of the world's oldest profession. Our ideas about legalisation of prostitution, which has generally happened in Western countries since the 1970s, have been very much influenced by Shaw's play, although most people today would not know the effect the play had back in 1892.

*St Joan* is another play by Shaw that has met with critical acclaim. The following speech is made to the Inquisition shortly before she is burnt at the stake. This is an example of Shaw's technique of embedding speeches of serious content into a comedy. Joan has realised that signing a confession will not give her freedom: she will live, but will spend her life in jail.

Joan tears up her confession, saying:

*St Joan*
by Bernard Shaw
Constable & Company 1932

JOAN: Yes: they told me you were fools (*the word gives great offence*), and that I was not to listen to your fine words nor trust to your charity. You promised me my life; but you lied (*indignant exclamations*). You think that life is nothing but not being stone dead. It is not the bread and water I fear: I can live on bread: when have I asked for more? It is no hardship to drink water if the water be clean. Bread has no sorrow for me, and water no affliction. But to shut me from the light of the sky and the sight of the fields and flowers; to chain my feet so that I can never again ride with the soldiers nor climb the hills; to make me breathe foul damp darkness, and keep from me everything that brings me back to the love of God when your wickedness and foolishness tempt me to hate Him: all this is worse than the furnace in the Bible that was heated seven times. I could do without my warhorse; I could drag about in a skirt; I could let the banners and the trumpets and the knights and soldiers pass me and leave me behind as they leave the other women, if only I could still hear the wind in the trees, the larks in the sunshine, the young lambs crying through the healthy frost, and the blessed blessed church bells that send my angel voices floating to me on the wind. But without these things I cannot live; and by your wanting to take them away from me, or from any human creature, I know that your counsel is of the devil, and that mine is of God.

*St Joan* begins with an apparently silly scene about chickens not laying eggs, and ends with a scene in heaven in which Joan is informed of her canonisation by the Church in 1920, nearly 500 years after her execution. How should you treat her speech? Should you treat it as you would a naturalistic play?

The first step is a basic analysis of the text, which will show you that Shaw's language is often more like Shakespeare's than like natural speech. In fact you could write the speech out like a kind of poetry:

Bread has no sorrow for me, and water no affliction.

But to shut me from the light of the sky

And the sight of the fields and flowers;

Craig Higgs as John Worthing, Jade Camden as Lady Bracknell, and Letitia Sutherland as Gwendolen Fairfax in the CSU production of Oscar Wilde's *The Importance of Being Earnest*. (Photo: Lee Verall)

To cháin my féet so that I can néver ríde agáin

With the sóldiers nor clímb the hílls;

To máke me bréathe foul damp dárkness,

And kéep from me éverything that brings me

    báck to the lóve of Gód

When your wíckedness and fóolishness tempt

    me to hate hím:

Áll this is wórse than the fúrnace in the Bíble

That was héated séven tímes.

Shaw, like Shakespeare, uses a pentameter as his baseline. His line structure, however, is less predictable and reflects the changes in poetry since Shakespeare's time. For example, in this speech he uses 3-stress and 6-stress lines which sometimes create for the modern audience an effect rather like an imitation of Shakespeare but which is not as 'musical'. (Shaw was influenced by Mozart but also very much by Wagner whose music is comparatively less easy on the ear.)

When you look for emotional through lines in Shaw's speech, you will notice that it is difficult to find lines that progress and cross to create shift points. The speech is more like a continuous blast at the same level of emotional intensity, and Joan's view of herself and the other doesn't change. This is the big difference between Shaw's writing and both naturalistic writing and Shakespeare.

Shaw's speeches have a dramatic structure, but he works at shifting the audience's feelings and thoughts without creating deeply felt characterisation. He uses the timing of comedy: pauses are deliberately lengthened to wait for the audience to get the gag. In this way he was the first of the English expressionist writers of the 20th century. We'll see later how Bertolt Brecht went on from where Shaw left off, but for now, let's look at how to prepare a Shaw speech for an audition.

## EXERCISE 26: AUDIENCE RESPONSE ANALYSIS IN SHAW

Read the speech through in the role of George Bernard Shaw, the writer. What do you want the audience to feel at the beginning of the speech

1. about the character who is speaking?
2. about the character(s) they are speaking to?

For example, you may decide that Shaw wanted the audience to feel that Joan is a fool to have torn up her confession and that Ladvenu and the Inquisitor are really doing their best to help her. Therefore the audience would feel fear for Joan, and sympathy for Ladvenu as she begins 'Yes: they told me you were fools.'

Now imagine what you want the audience to feel at the end of the speech as Joan says:

> But without these things I cannot live; and by your wanting to take them away from me, or from any human creature, I know that your counsel is of the devil, and that mine is of God.

For example, you may not want the audience to think that Joan is a fool. They should no longer fear for her, although they know she is going to be killed, as her faith is undeterred. At the same time, the audience may still feel the same level, or perhaps even more, sympathy for the Inquisitor, as he has to go through with the execution which he had hoped to avoid.

Draw a graph showing the two lines of change in the audience's feelings. As you do so, search for the lines where a shift in feeling takes place. For example, in the line 'But without these things I cannot live', the audience feels the intensity of Joan's faith, and also senses the impossibility of her situation: she will 'die' in jail though she lives; if she is executed she will die—yet live in the hereafter according to her faith.

After you have worked through the speech in the role of the writer, you need to switch to the role of actor as a communication technician.

## EXERCISE 27: CREATING THE EFFECT IN SHAW

Mark out the beats, the lengths of the pauses, the volume and the patterns of pitch that will create the feelings in the audience that you are aiming for. As you do this, you will find that the level of intensity is not as rigid as it originally seemed when you applied a standard character emotional through-line to the speech.

One reading would be:

(*abruptly*) Yes: | (*3 secs pause, then loudly*) they told me | (*short pause and then softer*) you were | (*1 sec pause then louder*) fools.

This manner of speaking would antagonise her opponents, and make the audience feel that Joan was putting herself at unnecessary risk.

This is a highly technical exercise and at first the result may seem too exaggerated, especially as you are used to working naturalistically. If you are working on your own, try recording your attempts on tape. As you give the speech, focus your attention outward towards your audience (through the microphone) rather than on your character. When listening back, listen the way you would to a piece of music, absorbing the sounds and how they make you feel.

With practice, you will be able to swing the audience's feelings as you go from phrase to phrase, and in doing so you will have learned what I call expressive acting. Shaw's plays were the first to require this style of conscious acting (although there was a long expressive tradition in circus clowning and the Commedia dell' Arte of Italy which links Shaw with Shakespeare's time).

When you understand how Shaw's writing is different from naturalistic writing, you will no longer find his plays too 'wordy'. They are, in fact, extraordinarily lively when played expressively and when his ideas come through clearly.

The qualities of each character in Shaw's plays are defined by their habits of language. An audition speech taken from any good play requires you to know the whole play so that you can prepare the speech in a way that makes sense within the context of its play (even though different directors will find different interpretations).

In a naturalistic script, your character needs to have a psychological consistency, based on their emotional responses to situations. Shaw creates the effect of psychological consistency through the character's language—word choice, intonation, pausing.

These can be used for comic exaggeration or to show more depth of character. A change of understanding in a character can be shown by a change in language. A good example is Sergius, from *Arms and the Man*. Sergius is a simple man who speaks in formulas to cover up his intellectual weakness. His famous line is 'I never apologise!'. In the final scene he realises that Bluntschli is the right person to marry Raina, not himself. Though he still uses a conventional line, when Sergius asks of Raina 'What says the lady?' his normal bombast softens: for the first time, he is asking for a real answer.

Shaw even gives Sergius the last line of the play, where instead of saying his usual self-centred 'I never apologise!' he expresses his unabashed admiration for Bluntschli: 'What a man! Is he a man!'

If this line is played with nothing but Sergius's old bombast, it can gain a laugh, but this is not really as good as Shaw deserves for the ending of his play. If the actor plays the line as if Sergius is genuinely stunned by Bluntschli's ability, lowering the volume and pitch of the final phrase and stressing 'he', his speech finally breaks his usual formula and the play takes on the full meaning as even Sergius comes to a new understanding.

There is nothing, if you search for emotional through-lines, in Sergius's character before this point to suggest that he will change. Shaw manipulates the change in the audience's feelings through the shift in Sergius' language.

## EXERCISE 28: SHAPING THE CHARACTER IN SHAW

Analyse Joan's language, from the beginning of the play through to her final speech before going to heaven. In what ways has her language changed in her final speech? What changes in her tone suggest a change in her understanding, and would make the audience sympathetic to her faith?

It may be useful to compare Joan's language in the following speech from Scene 3 with that in the Epilogue.

JOAN: (*matter-of-fact*) I will never take a husband. A man in Toul took an action against me for breach of promise; but I never promised him. I am a soldier: I do not want to be thought of as a woman. I will not dress as a woman. I do not care for the things women care for. They dream of lovers, and of money. I dream of leading a charge, and of placing the big guns. You soldiers do not know how to use the big guns: you think you can win battles with a great noise and smoke.

You will notice that when she is in heaven, Joan's language is more maternal and less domineering in tone. When she is in heaven, there is no threat to her faith and her language is able to become easy and relaxed in a way that wasn't possible on earth. Some directors feel that Joan's language in the Epilogue is inconsistent with her character and do not present the scene comfortably, or at all. However, omitting this scene destroys the message that Shaw sent his audience in 1924: in heaven, the humble Joan is equal with the King. Heaven on earth comes about only when all people are equal.

Shaw demonstrates his theme directly in his characters' language. He is a technician in words—just heaven for an actor.

## Bertolt Brecht

Bertolt Brecht had his first play produced in Germany in the 1920s. He left Nazi Germany to live in the

United States of America, returning to Communist East Germany after World War II. He is famous for such plays as *The Threepenny Opera*, *Mother Courage and Her Children*, *The Caucasian Chalk Circle* and *The Life of Galileo*. He wrote with the help and cooperation of many people including Elizabeth Hauptmann and the composer Kurt Weill.

Like Shakespeare and Shaw, Brecht's playwriting broke with tradition. His theories on playwriting had a great effect on theatre in the 20th century. He believed that the function of theatre was to challenge people intellectually, rather than manipulate them emotionally. His plays challenged the conventional emotional response of the audience, and aimed to extend that response into the reality beyond theatre. His theory of *Verfremdungseffekte*, (which is usually translated into 'Alienation Effect'), encouraged the audience to critically detach from what they were seeing on stage, rather than emotionally connect with the characters. I prefer to call this theory 'Distancing Effect', as it was an extension of Expressionism, such as we have seen in Shaw's work. Brecht, however, used less comedy than Shaw, or rather he played comedy with a black edge. As he witnessed the collapse of society and his homeland become a totalitarian dictatorship, Brecht and his friends could not accept even the comfort of a Shaw play which still let people off lightly in comparison with the reality outside the theatre.

## EXERCISE 29: SYLLAPHONES, BEATS, PAUSES AND STRESS PATTERNS IN BRECHT

Analyse the syllaphones, beats and pauses and look for the stress patterns in the following speech.

*The Caucasian Chalk Circle*
by Bertolt Brecht
Methuen Student Edition 1984

GRUSHA *to the child*. You mustn't mind the wind. It's only
a poor wretch, too. It has to push the clouds, and it
feels the cold more than any of us. *Snow starts falling*.
And the snow isn't the worst, Michael. It covers the
little fir trees, so they won't die in winter. And now I'll
sing you a little song. Listen! *She sings:*

> Your father's a thief
> Your mother's a whore:
> All the nice people
> Will love you therefore.
> The son of a tiger
> Brings the foals their feed
> The snake-child milk
> To mothers in need.

Most of the prose is in a 3-stress rhythm, which makes the language sound as if it has been cut short. This is not because it has been translated from its original German: Brecht and the people who have controlled his estate since 1956 only approved translations that were consistent with his style and intentions.

The song is even more blunt in style, with 2-stress lines which sounds like a simple march to a regular drum-beat. If you think now about the situation and the content of the words, you will see that nothing fits together in the conventional way: the wind is not powerful, but is a 'wretch' that 'feels the cold'; the snow is not cold, but keeps the fir trees warm; the situation for Grusha and the child seems terrible, yet she sings a song; and the song is for the child, but mentions the worst aspects of life instead of being a comfort.

This is how Brecht creates his distancing effect. Like Shaw, his aim is to swing the audience's responses (rather than create natural-seeming characters), but he goes one step further than Shaw.

Shaw uses his characters, rather like Shakespeare, to show how people outwit one another. His style of writing engages the audience in the lives of the characters, leaving the audience to think about the main ideas of the play when it has finished. Brecht, however, constantly reminds the audience that what they are watching is distanced from reality, ensuring that the audience considers the play's ideas while actually watching it.

## EXERCISE 30: REVERSAL WORDS IN BRECHT

Mark out the beats and pauses in Grusha's speech. Then find the beats where the words after the beat contradict our normal expectation (a reversal). For example:

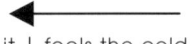

⬅———

...and it | feels the cold

(How can the wind feel the cold which it causes?) Present the speech as if you are explaining important information to the child, keeping your tone as factual as possible. Then present the speech entirely emotionally, with the feelings that you would experience if you were in Grusha's situation.

Finally, put these two presentations together: present Grusha's feelings and explanation. This is rather like working two emotional through lines.

Hopefully you will have found as you do this exercise that your focus is on your skills as an actor. If you manage to combine these two different approaches, the effect is highly dramatic. It forces the audience not just to identify with Grusha's feelings, but to also face the facts of her situation.

## EXERCISE 31: SINGING THE SONG IN BRECHT

Using the tune of *Baa, Baa, Black Sheep,* put a beat in each line to emphasise each reversal word:

> thief
>
> whore
>
> nice
>
> love
>
> tiger
>
> feed
>
> milk
>
> need

Sing the song so that the beats break up the strict rhythm, and then play with the presentation of the song until you can make it sound like an improvised piece of jazz (bring in some good musicians if you can).

You will have probably found that by the time you have done this exercise, you have forgotten about Grusha and the baby: you have become a singer working your audience as you would in a nightclub. In fact, it was in this sort of setting that Brecht and Kurt Weill originally conceived the new form of theatre, and today, in Australia, drama often takes place in pubs where a crowd of young people will gather rather than go to a formal (and expensive) theatre.

In going from Grusha's speech to her song, your position as an actor has changed from the presentation of a character talking to a baby (which is represented by a doll on stage, not a real child) to being an actor/singer entertaining an audience (even though you are still in costume as Grusha and holding the child). The effect is to make the audience very much aware that you are an actor playing roles. They cannot immerse themselves in apparently real characters. They are continuously confronted with the disparity between reality and the actors playing roles—the distancing effect.

Brecht's plays make people think, even as they watch, about the way people play roles all the time in real life, manipulating and being manipulated. You are not left to think things through after you leave the theatre as you are with Shaw's work. Nor are you able to leave the theatre just feeling sorry for a character (like Ibsen's Nora in *A Doll's House*) without needing to think about the situation too much.

By the end of *The Caucasian Chalk Circle*, you cannot help but realise how people are forced into situations where they have to do the wrong thing to survive, and that it is therefore unethical to put people in those situations.

From the actor's point of view, the value of Brecht's work is to focus attention on the actor as a skilled professional—his work is one of the reasons you are auditioning for professional training, and why expressionist acting is now part of our culture.

## Shakespeare, Shaw, Brecht—and back to naturalism

By working through the techniques I've suggested for these three playwrights, you will have realised, I hope, that there is not a rigid boundary between naturalism and expressionism.

Some plays, such as performance texts, are created entirely by improvising and workshopping, resulting in far more extreme expressionistic forms than Brecht created. A good collection of Australian work appears in *performing the unNameable* (edited by Richard James Allen and Karen Pearlman, Currency Press 1999).

Other plays, often coming out of community theatre companies, may emphasise naturalism. A good example is *Luck of the Draw* by Rosemary John which grew out of the Performing Ensemble of the Murray River Performing Group at Albury-Wodonga.

# EXERCISE 32: NATURALISM

Your last exercise, before the audition, is to prepare the following speech.

*Luck of the Draw*
by Rosemary John
Currency Press, 1986

RICHARD: How many times do we have to go over this? They don't know. They just read the little words in their little books ... They're the blokes who didn't go. They waved the placards, played the guitars. There we are, seven thousand miles away and there's Jim Bloody Cairns sitting in the middle of the road. No letters, no Christmas parcels: they're all piled up on the wharves because the fucking posties and wharfies didn't want to send them. And how did we feel? We felt bloody awful. They didn't care about us then and they certainly don't care now. Let's sweep it under the carpet, forget about it. All they care about are their cars, their jobs, where the next screw is coming from. I got one letter—one—in two months. I didn't ask to start a war with Vietnam, but I went because my marble came up in the lottery ... but they didn't think about that when they stopped our fucking letters. Don't you see? Your letters were my link with you and my life here.

{DIANNE: Sweetheart, that was fifteen years ago.}

RICHARD: Listen to me: do you know what terrified me over there? That I missed you and my friends more than they missed me. I lost two years of my life; it was like I didn't exist. While I was there, all I wanted was to sleep in my house, watch my TV and walk down the street with my wife. I remember arriving at the airport thinking, 'I'm safe, they can't blow me up now'. We didn't expect cheers, we didn't want thank yous, but it was midnight, we were whisked away. We were an embarrassment, to be hidden, and fifteen years later we still are.

# SCENE 6
# Research

It is important for you to remember that most auditions include an interview which can often be the deciding factor when there are many people who are talented and suitable for the course. You must prepare yourself as well as possible for this interview, which means researching your parts, theatre history, and the technical theory of theatre.

## Researching your parts

For each piece which you expect to present for an audition, you should know about the rest of the script and have ideas about why you have chosen to present it the way you do. When you are preparing an audition piece, you should ask the following questions about the play:

- Is the play naturalistic, expressionist or some other form?
- Is the shift point in this speech the turning point in the play (naturalism)?
- What change in understanding (for your character; or for the audience) happens during this speech?
- What different styles or themes might different directors use for this play?

If you are able to answer these questions you will be able to cope with the practical parts of your audition. For example, you won't be fazed by the auditioners asking you to present the speech in a different style from your original way of doing it, or if they ask you to justify why you did it the way you did.

If after working through the exercises in this book you find it difficult to answer these questions, you might seriously consider not auditioning for tertiary training at this stage, even though you may have a natural talent for acting or technical work.

This does not mean the end of your theatre career, but I suggest that you could be better off supporting yourself in some other way and taking part in practical theatre as an amateur. Some people find themselves well satisfied in amateur theatre where their income doesn't depend on their theatre work. Some people find that a few years in adult amateur theatre helps them gain the experience they need to do well in auditions for tertiary training.

## Researching theatre history

Researching theatre history is a lifetime activity for you as a professional. The following books are a good start:

Peter Holloway *Contemporary Australian Drama*
Leonard Radic *The State of Play*

John West *Theatre in Australia*
Eric Irvin *Theatre Comes to Australia*
Julian Meyrick *See How it Runs: Nimrod and the New Wave*
Cesare Molinari *Theatre Through the Ages*
Bamber Gascoigne *World Theatre*
Oscar G. Brockett *The Theatre: An Introduction*
J.L. Styan *Modern Drama in Theory and Practice*

If you are keen to read an academic journal which focuses very much on the practical nature of theatre, you can subscribe to *Australasian Drama Studies*.

There are many books of this kind. In your research you should be careful not to accept old-fashioned or racist ideas about theatre. For example, many books talk of theatre before Ancient Greek times, or theatre from oral cultures, as 'primitive'. Most books in English have a strong bias towards the Western theatre tradition, as if theatre in India, China, Japan or other places which have an equally long history are of little or no importance.

You should have a good general knowledge on the following topics if you wish to work in Australian theatre:

- British, European and American traditions which have been an important influence on mainstream theatre in Australia;
- Australian Indigenous traditions and the movement of Aboriginal theatre into the mainstream;
- Asian theatre and dance;
- the development of theatre which represents particular minority groups, lifestyles or viewpoints, such as Gay Theatre and Feminist Theatre; and
- the issues which divide theatre in Australia, such as government funding for community or

mainstream theatre; for State flagship companies or smaller innovative companies; for one-off projects or for permanent companies.

You will not easily find books which deal with the full range of research you should be doing. It makes more sense to take up your own interest in a particular area and check out newspaper archives, use the internet to find sources in the National Library of Australia, university libraries and the Virtual Library, and seek out theatre people with similar interests.

History is in a constant state of flux. Theatre is art which needs to keep creating new ideas and new ways of performing, although theatre also needs bums on seats and official subsidy. To me this means that having an interest in theatre history means you know when you are doing something new, but your knowledge of theatre history should never stop you from working at what you think is important and relevant to do today.

## Research into technical skills

You might finish secondary school as a good actor, singer, dancer, lighting or sound technician, and yet you may not realise that you are able to do this mainly because you are good at solving certain problems which are thrown at you.

For example, my sense of colour was never as good as my sense of timing. This means that I am naturally very good at using pauses when acting, and very good at operating lighting. But make-up, costume and lighting design—where using colours and being able to create interesting effects are essential—are areas of weakness for me.

You should honestly examine your own strengths and

weakness and focus your skills research to add new skills to your repertoire and to support your work with more knowledge. This research will fall into two kinds:

- Taking classes in specialist skills, such as: fencing; dance (including folk, period dance, modern, ballroom, tap, jazz etc.); voice (speaking voice, singing); mime; make-up; costume-making; set design and construction; lighting design; sound mixing; electronics; electrical safety.
- Studying the theory behind the practical skills, for example: colour mixing in light and pigment; tension and release in dance and movement; the anatomy of voice production; theatre acoustics (for voice, live music, audio amplification); semiotics and notation—the symbolic representation of theatre, movement and dance in performance.

There are many more possibilities. Skills research, like your research into theatre history, will never come to an end, and more than likely will be driven by what you need for a particular situation—a training exercise, an audition, a role in a production.

The main point about research is that you should keep yourself open to all possibilities. In some areas of the arts, you can be a specialist (let's say in printmaking) and by focussing on that one area you become more and more skilled and, hopefully, recognised and financially successful. Theatre arts is a broad and ever-changing area of human endeavour. The more you learn through study and experience, across the range of theatre work, the more your special talents can shine.

And now we move on to your opportunity to shine: Act 4: The audition.

# ACT 4
# The audition

## SCENE 1
## Warming up

Where and when is your audition—in Sydney, Melbourne, Perth, Canberra, Toowoomba, Adelaide, Brisbane, Launceston, Townsville, Wagga Wagga ... at 9am?

Are you prepared to travel and stay over night before and one or even two nights after? Just organising the timetable if you are auditioning for several different places, and finding the money, can be a hassle. Of course, theatre life is a continuous rearrangement of time and place. Get used to it now: make sure you get all the information as early as you can from each institution. If there are clashes, get back to people and make other arrangements.

Act 5: Epilogue will give you some information on the range of courses that are available in Australia. It's much more sensible to select the training courses which suit you, even if they are far away, than to only audition close to home for less suitable courses. You are more likely to succeed in auditions this way, and more likely to find the course you end up in more satisfying. The first stage of warming up is planning ahead as much as possible.

### Structure of the day

If it is possible, visit the venue the day before the audition (or earlier, remembering that the space may be in use). If you can get inside to study the layout, the acoustics and the general feel of the space where the auditions are held, this will help you know how to adjust your presentation to suit. Is the space warm and inviting, cold and forbidding, acoustically lively or dead? Whatever you find, prepare yourself to work with the venue: use its advantages and work out how to overcome its problems.

Check out where you will be while waiting—outside in the sunshine, in a cold corridor, in the auditorium while others do their pieces?

Find out the way auditions are organised. Are they, for example,
- individual calls with a call back after the first piece if you're accepted at this stage?
- group movement and voice warm-up session followed by pair work and individual calls?
- interview before presenting an audition?
- call back with interview on the second day?

There are many variations, and they change from place to place and year to year. Act 5: Epilogue contains current or recent information, but make sure you check with the institution before you arrive so you know, to some extent, what to expect.

## On the day

So you have a 9am call. What does that tell you about the audition? Maybe everyone called on that day is taken in for a pep talk or a group warm-up session. Almost certainly you'll get a good idea at this point of the day's timetable—and you can bet that there will be large black holes of time that you'll need to fill in: before your presentation, between sessions, and hopefully after your first day's auditions if there is a call back for selected people the next day. The waiting time can be worse than the audition, unless you prepare yourself thoroughly.

What do you do in these periods of time? Do you forget all your experience in drama classes and feel anxious or angry? Well, sometimes the answer is yes to either or both. One of my successful students became furious with me when I deliberately kept her waiting, but after she had begun her tertiary training she understood why I had forced her to face reality. Her anger gave her such energy and determination, and she realised that this had been the key to her success.

Think about how you work:

- Do you need to build up energy to make your presentation stand out?
- Do you need to calm yourself and focus yourself on the task ahead in a quiet way, ready to make your performance fully realised?
- Can you prepare yourself for your theatre work in a public space, where you don't have the protection and comfort of a theatre?

## EXERCISE 33: WARM-UP EXERCISE

You will know from past experience which exercises work for you. Choose one to do while you are waiting for your call up. Perhaps the most common format is stretching large muscles first (torso, thighs); loosening limbs and joints (shoulders, elbows, wrists, hips, knees, ankles); neck and spine stretches and gentle loosening; diaphragm breathing; balance and centring; voice.

In a public situation, where a physical warm-up may attract unwelcome attention, use breathing and visualisation without being obvious. While maintaining diaphragm breathing (short breath in, long breath out), you can visualise the stretching and loosening you would normally perform, including even the voice exercises. Some people find that purely mental preparation like this relaxes them more than a physical warm up. If you need a book, I have found *The Actor at Work* by Robert Benedetti very useful (see Act 5: Epilogue, References).

As well as having warm-up exercises ready to use when you need them, you also need to think about other factors during waiting times:

- Do you benefit from lots of communication with other people, or are you better off isolating yourself so you aren't distracted?
- Are you better off deliberately distracting yourself, because taking your mind off having to wait and what might happen means you can be fresh when you are called?

Perhaps you could check out the coffee shops and bars, or take an engrossing book, or seek out spaces where you can do some yoga, or join in with other people in light-hearted games, or some serious improvisations—or whatever. Do whatever works best for you, but make sure that you are prepared to fill in time while you are waiting for your call up.

## SCENE 2
### Taking the stage

This scene is about how you take control of the space in which you are going to perform, and discover some 'rules' about movement in space and the visual impact you will have upon your audience.

Remember what you learned in Act 1: the auditioners are affected by what they see long before you begin acting your role. How you walk on to the acting area and where you stand will have an impact.

I'm going to describe what you should do for a more traditional situation than you may find yourself in. The principles, however, may be adjusted to suit the various situations that you will face during different auditions.

## EXERCISE 34: TAKING THE STAGE

As in Act 1, imagine that I am seated halfway along one side of a rectangular space, such as a studio area. If the space is not square, then I would be on the longer wall. Alternatively, imagine me seated in the middle of the second row of seats in a conventional proscenium theatre.

Choose a spot along the up-down centre line of the space, towards the down end (i.e. towards me) where you will make an announcement about who you are and what your audition piece will be.

Experiment with going 'off stage' (which might be to the side of the space or in the wings) and walking to your chosen spot along different lines of movement:

- start from upstage left and right, centre left and right, downstage left and right;
- walk in a straight line;
- try a curved line towards downstage before going to your announcement position;
- try a curved line towards upstage before going to your announcement position.

What did you find?

Without an audience to give you feedback, you may have felt more comfortable using a curved line of movement. This will give you time to take in your surroundings and make your presence known, whereas

## ENTERING ALONG STRAIGHT LINES

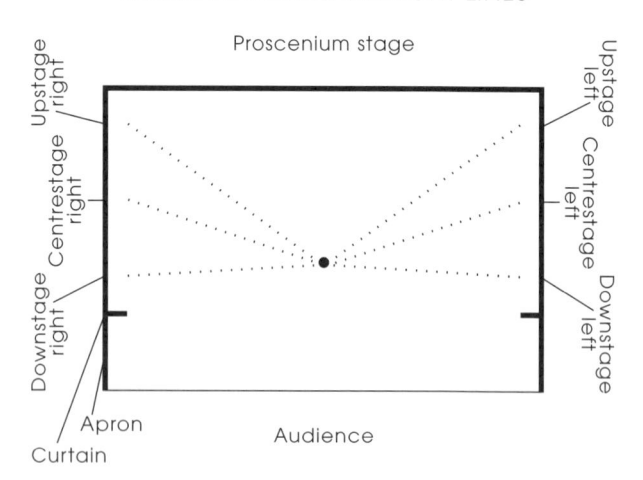

Proscenium stage

- Upstage right
- Centrestage right
- Downstage right
- Apron
- Curtain
- Upstage left
- Centrestage left
- Downstage left

Audience

## ENTERING ALONG POSITIVE CURVED LINES

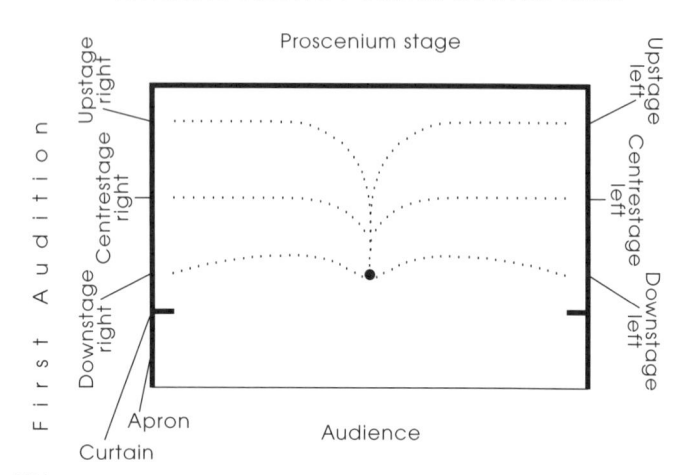

Proscenium stage

- Upstage right
- Centrestage right
- Downstage right
- Apron
- Curtain
- Upstage left
- Centrestage left
- Downstage left

Audience

First Audition

a straight line may feel too abrubt.

You may also have noticed, especially if you imagined me watching you, that the entrance which gives you the best feeling of control of the situation is to begin from upstage left or right and use a curve which keeps you upstage, gradually coming down and towards your announcement position. The graphs on page 104 demonstrate the various entrances. If you have an audience, they will confirm that a positive curve from upstage is the best entrance.

A straight line walk to the announcement spot can seem very quick, peremptory and even threatening to the audience, especially when you start from upstage. Entering from downstage gives the audience only a profile, and perhaps even a partial back view as you move to your announcement spot. Both of these approaches leave a negative impression.

Using a curve gives the audience a much warmer feeling than a straight line, but a negative curve (towards downstage before reaching your announcement spot) presents even more of your back view if you start downstage, and can seem even more threatening if you start upstage.

When I mentioned 'rules' before, you should be clear that we are working here with how people feel in response to your movement and position in space, so you can't take the advice I'm giving you too rigidly. When you are in the real situation, you must sense what feels best in that space at that time.

You should make your positive curve stay longer upstage before turning down centre, but it shouldn't become a straight line until the last few steps to your announcement spot.

When you enter from upstage, on a gentle curve towards the centre and down to your announcement spot, your audience will know that you can see all the stage from the moment you enter. They will be able to see a well rounded figure from profile to full frontal, and the curved movement feels warm and leaves a positive impression. It gives them time to assess what they see, and you time to sense the atmosphere. Provided you don't come too far downstage, your audience will feel comfortable and certainly not threatened by you.

Now you are ready to begin. Remember I will describe the most formal situation. You may only need to use some of the points from the next few scenes, but the principles will be useful even in informal auditions.

## SCENE 3
## The introduction

The introduction consists of announcing who you are (remember the first exercise in Act 1) and the part you are going to perform.

### Downstage centre

Where should you be on the stage? (For now I shall assume you are on a conventional proscenium stage). The formal 'rule' is that you should be centre stage, a little downstage from the 'strong' positions. This is because your announcement is out of role, and you will want to move into one of the strong positions to present your role.

### The strong positions

Where are the 'strong' positions?

My stories about how these positions came to be

recognised have been passed down from European theatre traditions. I don't know how true they are, but every time I have worked with people exploring these ideas, everyone has responded the same way.

The artists of the Renaissance period had a great interest in perspective. Medieval paintings look two dimensional, but later artists attempted to make their work three dimensional.

The first step was to realise that the lines which represent parts of the picture going further away from the viewer should all end at, or point to, a single point on the horizon. At first this point was placed in the centre of the picture. It has become known as the vanishing point.

However, though this looks more three dimensional than early medieval painting, it still looks distorted. As mathematics was also a passion of the Renaissance, 'golden rules' were discovered.

The first golden rule was that the best shape for an architectural landscape was a rectangle which is around 5 units wide by 4 units high. You'll see this on your computer if you choose the landscape setting in your word processor. You'll also notice that a good proscenium stage, when viewed from the centre of the seating, gives a picture which is close to those proportions.

The second golden rule was that the vanishing point of perspective seemed to draw the viewer's attention much more strongly if, instead of being in the centre, it was positioned at any one of four points in the painting: one third in from either side, and one third in from top or bottom edge.

As soon as you think about (or preferably go and look at) a stage, you'll realise that it is already in three dimensions, unlike a flat painting. A stage also doesn't have such definite borders as a painting. And yet it is still true that the 5 by 4 rule and the one third rule work on stage. You just have to move around until you feel right, rather than do strict measurements, as the extra open spaces, the dark areas and even different colours and lights affect your sense of space and its shape. (By the way, maybe this is the problem with the Sydney Opera House Drama Theatre stage—it is too wide for its height so the one third rule doesn't work properly.)

## Strong points

A conventional proscenium stage which is in the right proportions has twelve strong points:

- one third in from left and right and one third in from upstage and downstage edges (4 positions);
- one third up from the stage floor, and in from L, R, US, DS (4 positions); and
- one third down from the top of the set, and in from L, R, US, DS (4 positions)

If you try drawing a picture of the stage from the audience's viewpoint, an interesting thing you will notice is that the head of a person standing on a strong point is just about at one third up from the floor. If you stand a person on a rostrum one third up from the floor, their head will just about be at the strong point one third down from the top of the set. So in effect you really have only eight strong positions to work with: four on the floor and four at one third up rostrum height. Standing on a rostrum two thirds high places the person's head at the top of the set, and the strength of the position is lost (though sitting, squatting or lying down at this position can still work).

# STRONG POINTS AND ANNOUNCEMENT SPOT

Proscenium stage

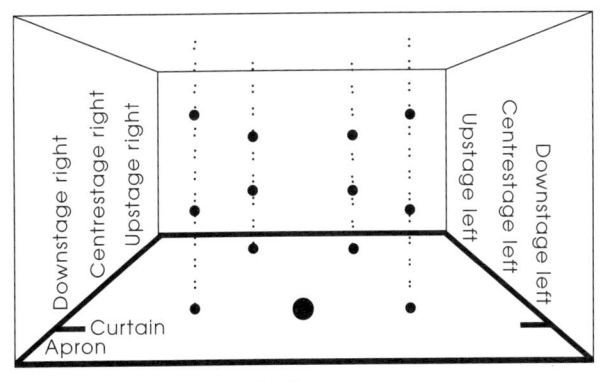

Audience

## The strongest position

Where is the strongest position? This introduces my favourite, and probably apocryphal story, about the French King Louis XIV, (or, as he preferred to call himself, the Sun King).

Before the story, you should try taking each of the four strong points on the stage floor, spending some time in each position and sensing how you feel as you turn about and imagine interacting with other people on stage.

If you have other people there to test out your reactions, you should notice that people who are further downstage than you are in a weaker position. Even though they are closer to the audience, you have the upper hand because you can approach them from behind. The audience can see you and can sense that you can be a threat to the downstage actor.

This is what is meant when people talk of 'up-staging'

someone—the person up stage has the advantage. In the period of European theatre history when the audience sat on a flat floor and the stage was raked, the back of the stage was literally up compared with the front of the stage which was lower, so that all the audience could see all the actors. Nowadays it is usual to build the stage flat and rake the seating—but the visual effect, and the audience's reactions, are the same.

If you have had to perform in one of those awful school halls where both the stage and the auditorium have flat floors, you'll know the frustrating problem of actors 'blocking' each other, and how hard it is to make an impact from the back of the stage, yet the upstage actor still has an emotional advantage over the downstage actor.

Which of the two upstage strong points is the stronger? Try them out for a while and see how you feel. Most of my students have felt that the upstage right position is the strongest; though quite a few have gone for the upstage left. Sometimes (though, I have to admit, not consistently) the right-handed people have preferred upstage right and the left-handers preferred upstage left.

I've never checked out the truth of my story to see if King Louis XIV was actually right-handed, but this is the way the story goes.

King Louis was not only a strong supporter of theatre, he took part on stage himself—in fact he insisted on having the most important roles. Now, he lived in dangerous times, and did not want to put himself in a position where someone could assassinate him. Being right-handed, when he was on stage he had to be in a position where he was far enough away from the surrounding curtains to avoid someone attacking him with a sword from behind (this is called being stabbed through the arras) and he had to have everyone else on the stage in his sight and to his left.

With his sword on his left side, any untoward movement in the corner behind him could be dealt with by drawing his sword—with his right hand—and turning to his right. All the actors would be positioned too far on stage left and downstage to be able to mount an attack before he could defend himself. So, according to the story, whenever King Louis XIV performed, he took the strong position upstage right—and stayed there throughout the play! And this explains why the upstage right one-third-in position is the strongest on the stage.

### The announcement position

To make your announcement, enter from upstage right if possible, or upstage left if necessary. Move in a curved line through or close by the nearest upstage strong position, coming down to centre a little below the line between the downstage strong positions.

When you begin your performance, after your announcement, move to the downstage strong position on the side opposite to your entrance. This maintains a smooth line of movement and keeps your profile open to the audience.

Why not use King Louis' upstage position? On a large space with noone else on stage, it's lonely at the top, too far from your audience and too far to go after making your announcement. Yet you might find an upstage position will work in a small space or with a large audience, so keep it in mind.

### The announcement

We now come to the matter of what you should say when you announce who you are and what part you will perform. First of all, a reminder: I am describing the most formal situation. If the auditioners have already noted all the details, there may be no need to introduce yourself just before performing. They may call you on by name and ask you, for example, to perform Raina from *Arms and the Man*. In this case you can enter and take your position to perform without going to the downstage centre spot at all. You may find that a long curving entry in this situation is too long, and you may be better to begin performing from an upstage strong position and move down as part of the performance.

A second point about formality: in the most formal tradition, the actor should stand still while making an announcement—and, after moving to a performance position, should remain in that position with minimal movement while performing. In less formal auditions this may seem stilted, and you should feel free to move, so long as you take care not to create a negative or threatening feeling in your audience. If you can, check with the auditioners whether they prefer minimal movement or would like to see you use the stage area freely: different training schools have their own traditions on this point.

## EXERCISE 35: THE ANNOUNCEMENT

When you make an announcement, the aim is to be brief, to the point and clear. Following this aim, the formal 'rule' is to say:

> My name is Sheila Rowbotham. I shall perform

> Lavinia from *Mourning Becomes Electra* by Eugene O'Neill.

The formula is 'My name is (your name). I shall perform (your character's name) from (the name of the play) by (the author of the play)'.

There is no need to give any more explanation, unless the auditioners ask for further information. They won't need to, of course, if you have chosen a good speech from an established play. Many institutions ask you to choose contrasting pieces including, say, a Shakespeare, a modern piece, and both comedy and serious drama. The auditioners may ask you to present your Shakespeare, or your comedy piece. At this stage they may already know your name and you can say which piece you will perform without going through the formal motions. If you are asked to do two pieces in a row, you could announce them both and take a short break between each piece (even move from one strong point to another), or announce one and do it before announcing the second one and doing it.

The principle behind the formal announcement is don't waste words: if you say too much the announcement will get in the way of the performance.

Finally, remember your work in Act 1. When you make the announcement, you are not in character. This is the time when you appear on stage and speak as yourself, and it is important for the auditioners to see the genuine you. Use your warm-up skills so that you can present yourself clearly and effectively and let the auditioners see the person they will be working with for the next three years. If you are sincere and open at this time, and your performances suggest you have talent and have put work into developing your skills, then you are giving yourself the best chance of being accepted and succeeding in a professional training course.

## SCENE 4
### Transition from yourself to your role

In the formal situation, after you have made your announcement, you should move to the strong position left or right (opposite the side you entered from) and slightly upstage of your announcement position.

When you first try this move, it can be fraught with problems. It can seem a long way to go. If you turn upstage too much you lose your profile from the audience's point of view. Your feet can get tangled. And yet, if you practise it, this move can be just what is needed to give you the time to focus on your role, to recall your through-lines and other technical points you have prepared, so that by the time you turn to fully face your audience you are in control and in role.

To make the move successfully, follow these rules:
- Take no more than 4 steps—1, 2, 3 and turn.
- Don't worry about following the one-third rule exactly, moving towards the strong point will work. If you feel you need to, you can build moving into stronger positions as part of your performance.
- Keep as much of your profile towards the audience as you can, but focus more on preparing yourself for your role—your concentration will work to keep the audience's attention on you. They are now seeing you as performer moving into role and will respect your focus.

- Take your time—turn when you are ready to perform, and begin speaking only when the character needs to speak.

## SCENE 5
## Dramatic shape and audience reaction

You will, of course, have spent a long time finding through lines and shift points in your speech. Though you are presenting a short extract from a much longer play, in your audition this speech must have the same dramatic effect as if it were a complete play and you only have two minutes.

When you think about this, you'll understand that studying Shakespeare, Shaw and Brecht has a new importance. If you focus only on your character in a naturalistic way, your through lines and shifts may be as true to the character as anyone can imagine. However, it may not work with your audience when the speech is given out of its proper context, without the rest of the play. The more expressionist aspects of presenting Shaw or Brecht, which focus on the audience's response, will help you shape your speech—after all, even naturalism is a theatrical illusion.

When you are making your announcement, and at other times if you can, keep your wits about you. Observe the auditioners. Try to gauge how sensitive they are to naturalism or to stylised ways of performing. You may notice these things during a group movement warm-up or improvisation exercises. Unfortunately, the auditioners are not going to tell you in so many words what they think and feel—you will need to stick out your antennae and check what you receive.

As you move into position for your performance you'll need to focus on the task ahead in order to start at the right emotional level, but once your performance is under way let your attention go out towards your audience. I'm sure you will have experienced this when you have acted previously.

Whenever I am on stage, I see myself as three people working in a team. One of me is the actor creating the role. This me is focussed on the character's feelings, acting as if for naturalism, or on the language and its effects to create a Shakespearean, Shavian or Brechtian role. Another me is aware of sound, space and light (and the other actors in a full production): it's this me who tells me to move a bit upstage, downstage, left or right so a spotlight catches my eyes, or to make sure I am being heard, or to make eye contact with another actor. It's this me who usually tells me to move if I've been still too long; or to stay still because to move might break the atmosphere. My third person is aware of the feelings coming up from the audience—warm, excited, attentive, indifferent, cold, hostile. This is the me who tells me to give more to the audience, to add pauses so they can catch up with me, to change the way I would have said something so that I get a laugh to lighten the atmosphere. When these three aspects of myself work together I produce my best performance.

Working an audience of auditioners is possibly the hardest acting you'll ever have to do. They haven't paid to see you for entertainment—they are paid to judge your work. But remember that they are seeking potential professional actors. If things flag, don't be afraid to work hard to revive your scene. If things go over the top, don't be afraid to pull back, take a pause and let the scene settle back to where it should be. Your auditioners will recognise that you have sensed what they are feeling and that you have taken control.

Show your strengths as an actor by working intelligently, using your skills and techniques. In the audition competition it is not 'raw talent' which will get you into a tertiary training course, but your awareness of yourself, your role and your audience, and your willingness to adapt to the situation. In other words, your willingness to learn.

## SCENE 6
### Finish and exit

Leaving the stage when you have finished your performance is not a simple matter of turning away from your audience and disappearing as fast as possible. The 'rule' is to exit out of role in a dignified manner. This means that when your performance is finished you should pause to let the effect of the speech sink in. During this pause you should come out of role. Let yourself do this in your own time. You may need to use a brief 'warm down'—breathing and relaxation—and refocus your full attention on the ordinary reality around you.

This gives you time to check out whether you are expected to leave without further ado, or whether the auditioners have something to say immediately. If they say something like 'Thank you', take it as the signal to exit. If they begin to speak to you, or to each other about you, wait. If they say nothing, don't take this as a criticism—take the silence as a mark of respect for your work and exit.

When you exit from the performance area, stay within hearing in case the auditioners decide to call you back. Sometimes the auditioners need some time to think or confer with each other before asking you to discuss the piece you presented or to present it again with some specific instructions.

The immediate problem is how do you walk off stage 'in a dignified manner'. Like your entrance, a straight-line exit will seem cold and harsh. On the other hand a long curving line may seem too deliberate and time consuming.

If you have performed most of the time in one area, such as the downstage strong area opposite the side you entered from, and the only exit point is where you came in, then you have no choice: you have to turn away from centre and take a curve upstage and back to your entry point. That is, from the down stage right position, turn away to your right and then curve across and up stage to an upstage left exit.

If you can exit opposite your entry, then you can turn towards centre and upstage to exit.

It is generally better to exit upstage or at least at centre left or right, rather than downstage left or right, but you will have to judge the circumstances. On a very big stage a downstage exit is still long enough for dignity. Or you may be in a situation where the people auditioning sit in the auditorium and you need to exit down steps at the front of the stage. (In this situation, by the way, you would also have had to enter up these steps, and find a nicely shaped line to take you to your announcement or performance position).

The important point is to have a plan. If possible, check the area before you go on stage and decide how you will turn and exit. Otherwise, use the pause after you finish performing to make your decision and at the right moment follow your plan. You are yourself as you walk off, so focus on checking through the successful parts of the performance. (You could decide to exit in role as the speech ends, but this is a wimp's way out. You show much more strength of purpose if you stay and face your audience as yourself before leaving them to judge your work.)

Only when you are offstage and are not called back immediately should you indulge in analysing the less successful parts of your performance. This is a matter for Scene 8: Postmortem.

# SCENE 7
## Call back and interviews

Any sort of call back means that the auditioners have some interest in you. If, say, only fifteen people will be selected from 1500 applicants, it is obvious that calling back and interviewing is going to be the crunch time. Even if you do well at this stage, it doesn't guarantee success. It will be a matter of how well you do, in addition to a good performance, in comparison with all those other applicants.

If you felt nervous before presenting your audition pieces, this is the time you have every right to feel overwhelmed—unless you have prepared yourself well.

### Callback—character interpretation

You have presented your performances (or one piece) and the auditioner asks you to do it again, but with some new instructions. The auditioner's purpose is to see how you cope with being directed, how adaptable you are in presenting your character, how much you know about theatre.

The auditioner may give you an instruction that is designed to throw you off-balance—perhaps even physically. They may ask you to perform your piece with one arm held behind your back. You must keep your arm in a very uncomfortable position, yet present your character true to the part. Keep focussed on your through-line, adding the feeling of discomfort. If you are really good, your character will seem real and the audience will become unaware of the odd position of your arm. You may even be able to find a justification within the character for your arm being there.

There are many variations of this kind of instruction, including emotional arms behind your back. For example, say you have presented Coralie Lansdowne as an aware person who realises she has found the partner who suits her real needs. The auditioner asks you to present the piece again for a director who takes a black view of Buzo's work: he sees Coralie as subconsciously hating Stuart—her apparent awareness is simply another layer of falsehood in her character. Rather than *Coralie Lansdowne Says No* being a romantic comedy in which marriage has at least a reasonable chance of success, this director wishes to impose their bleak view that all marriage is doomed. Maybe this is a misogynist director, or an extreme feminist.

What do you do? You can see the auditioner is deliberately putting you in an unfair situation, but you can take the instruction on board and try it out. How much does Coralie hate Stuart at the beginning of the speech? How much by the end? Being unconscious of her hatred, does she seem to love him more at the very moment when her hate is greatest? Does this mean she hates herself, or feels more satisfied with herself the more she hates him? If the auditioner seems willing you could ask some of these questions before launching into the new Coralie who says 'yes' when she means 'no'. Otherwise go for it, and maybe the auditioner will ask you some questions afterwards, when you can explain what you did to find new emotional throughlines.

What is your purpose, then? To show the auditioner you can deal with unexpected, even contrary, instructions; and that you have techniques at hand to help you. To show, in other words, that you are an intelligent actor.

## Callback—theatrical form

The situation is similar—you are called back to do it again with new instructions—but this time your theatrical knowledge will be tested. 'Thank you, Rebecca. You presented a very effective naturalistic character. Would you now please do it again for a director who requires an entirely expressionist effect?'

Here is a challenging request: do you know enough to be able to switch your presentation from naturalism to expressionism? You would need to know more than the techniques I have suggested for handling Brecht. You will need to have studied expressionism as a theatrical form, use a technique which makes your character non-naturalistic, and be able to explain what you did and how it would be appropriate for this type of director.

You might, for example, study the rhythmic way of presenting lines, especially in Shakespeare's political plays, developed by the British director Steven Berkoff. At least you should have read a book such as *Modern Drama in Theory and Practice* by J.L.Styan (see Act 5: Epilogue, References) so that you know the difference between realism, naturalism, symbolism, surrealism, absurd theatre, expressionism and epic theatre. It's unlikely that anyone would be expected to understand all these thoroughly at the end of Year 12, but your auditions are open to anyone and to have some knowledge of these theatrical forms and be able to try ideas out in front of the auditioner will help at the beginning of tertiary professional training.

## Callback and interview—overview for acting and technical

It is traditional in some institutions to call actors back on the second day to present another performance and to face an interview. In some cases this might happen later on the same day. Information in Act 5: Epilogue should help you on this point, or tell you who to contact.

If you decide to apply for technical training, you should check out what you will be required to do at different institutions. In some courses, everyone works together in First Year, and you make choices from Second Year about concentrating on acting or technical. In other courses you make the choice when you first enrol. Some institutions also require everyone to include a statement or even a short essay with their application for theatre training, with an explanation of why they are applying.

In an interview, this is the main question: Why do you want to become an actor/lighting designer/costume designer/audio designer/ set designer/stage manager…?

The question is simple, but there is no 'correct' answer. You need to be thoroughly prepared so that if your performances or your set design models have got you through to an interview you can speak confidently about:

- what you want to achieve by working in theatre;
- what you already know about theatre practice; and
- your commitment to training and working.

Think carefully about what you want to achieve. For example:

- Is it that you enjoy theatre work, and want to have a life following your interest, with the main point being that by learning to be a better performer you will have better theatre experiences and enjoy the work even more? or
- Do you see working in theatre as important not only for yourself but for your audiences? Is providing good quality entertainment enough, or do you have other ideas about theatre—like how you can educate people or change their views politically?

Having a personal vision or a 'big picture' vision is not a matter of acceptable or unacceptable ideas (though it could be naïve to have 'becoming wealthy' as your goal, even though a few famous actors do make money). What's important is to have thought through your reasons for wanting to take on several years of professional training.

Gather together a collection of research information about theatre history; theatrical forms and styles; techniques for your area of interest in theatre; and the theatre workplace.

If you can't afford to buy many books, go through

the shelves of specialist bookshops and choose a few, with at least one each covering history, styles and techniques. Read as much as you can. Keep away from superficial theatrical gossip which really won't teach you anything new (the internet can be a trap—but there's lots of good information, too). Search out books, videos, tv and radio programs which are about things you didn't know about before. You will never finish reading and learning about theatre.

To learn about the theatre at work, you need to go out to commercial theatres and ask questions. How do Workplace Agreements and Awards operate when you are employed as an actor or technical operator? What trade union, if any, should you join? Should you have personal insurance cover in case you are injured while working or training? How much can you expect to be paid? Do you get paid the same for performing as you do when you are rehearsing? Do you need a solicitor to check over any contracts you have to agree to? How does Worker's Compensation work?

In this book it would be foolish of me to answer all these questions, because the answers keep changing. You should find out the answers, or you may find yourself working without pay or protection. You might not find it easy to say no, but you have the same rights in theatre work as you do in any other workplace. The references in Act 5: Epilogue include union and government agency contacts which you should find useful.

When you face an interview, any good auditioner will be trying to make a judgement about two main things. Firstly: Is your commitment to training backed up by your commitment to learning? Do you already know a lot about theatre and do you show a clear interest in learning more? (The person who is committed to doing the practical training but seems unlikely to take on the extra learning is less likely to be accepted.)

Secondly, is your commitment based on a realistic understanding of what it is like to work full time in theatre? Do you have clear plans for how you will support yourself through the training period and for working in an industry where most actors are 'resting' most of the time? (The person who unrealistically imagines only the exciting side of theatre work is less likely to be accepted.)

## EXERCISE 36: TEST OF KNOWLEDGE

Test yourself, without books or references, by writing down in point form as much as you can of what you know of

- Theatre History
- Theatre Forms and Styles
- Techniques for your area of interest in theatre
- The theatre workplace

Don't expect to be able to write down everything you have ever read about, but if this test takes you about an hour and you have something under each heading, then you have enough for a fair interview.

## EXERCISE 37: WRITTEN PRESENTATION

Write an essay of 1000 words on 'Why I want to work in theatre'.

Write a 500 word version of your essay, keeping the essential points.

Write a 300 word version with 100 words for each of the three main points.

## EXERCISE 38: ORAL PRESENTATION

Make a tape (video or audio) of your response to the question 'Why do you want to do theatre training?' Do this without books or references.

When you do this exercise remember your exercises in Act 1: Confrontation with your self and Act 3: The announcement. You are not acting during the interview—you are presenting yourself in the most effective way you can.

## SCENE 8
## Postmortem

Postmortem means 'after death'! It's the word usually used for the evaluation session after a production has finished its run. Make your evaluation objective. Check out where you think your techniques were successful and unsuccessful, and plan how you will work on improving for next time.

If you have not succeeded in being accepted for training, consider the whole of your situation carefully. It's not a good idea to starve for your art—in fact you'll need to be healthy and fit to have a chance at the next audition—so find a way to support yourself. Once you have had the experience of auditioning you'll know when you feel ready to try again. Maybe you'll be ready next year, or maybe you need a few years' experience before you audition again. Don't give up easily, but don't become a martyr.

Now that you have read and practised all the techniques I've suggested, from child-like playing with isolated sounds, through beats and through-lines, to taking the stage and presenting yourself, I need to tell you a story before you go.

Once, among a small audience, I heard a Tibetan lama spend an hour giving us the Tibetan Buddhist picture of the universe—from the heavenly waters on which floats the giant turtle, on whose back stand the four mighty elephants, on whose backs … until at the very pinnacle in eternal meditation the Buddha sits in the lotus position.

We were, of course, silent for the hour as image piled upon image and complex relationships were constructed.

When he finished, the silence continued—meditative, reverential, respectful of the lama's intellectual skills, cognisant of Tibetan Buddhism's wondrous image of the cosmos.

The lama took his time, perfectly judged, and in the silence grinned a little, then more broadly, and then with a comic face, he finally spoke. 'Don't believe a word of it', he said.

The tension relieved, of course the whole audience fell about laughing, taken in by an hour long joke.

Yet the lama's joke is full of truth. Buddhist philosophy explains that beliefs, such as the Tibetan cosmology, are the creation of our minds. We can never be free to reach nirvana until the mind realises that all it 'knows' is its own creation. At the moment of self-realisation (enlightenment) nirvana is achieved.

I don't aim to help you reach nirvana in this book, but I hope to help you on your way to better, hopefully great, acting. Like the lama's joke, I have to say to you that all the techniques I have offered you, and all those you will be taught or will pick up in the future, are nothing beside your own personality, talent and intuition. After all, the lama never went to NIDA. (Neither did Russell Crowe, but he still has an Oscar for best actor.)

For you to express yourself through acting, techniques (like mantras for meditation) are tools which you use naturally—as if you have never had to learn them. It's like speaking your lines: they must sound natural, as if they are coming directly from your character, not revealing that you had to spend hours memorising them.

Relying solely on technique, saying I know what to do and now I shall do it, will help you show your skills and intelligence. But it is not until you can say 'Don't believe a word of it' like the Tibetan lama that you will find yourself capital-A Acting.

I can't guarantee you success in your auditions. Noone can. But go in there and tell the ultimate joke, and you never know, you may be the chosen one.

'Oh what a beautiful sunrise': Andrew Hughes as Adam, Alison McMillan as Evelyn and Jade Camden as Georgie in the CSU production of *Baby X* by Campion Decent.

# APPENDIX A
## Act 5: Epilogue

### TERTIARY DRAMA/THEATRE/ PERFORMING ARTS COURSES AROUND AUSTRALIA

This listing is not a complete coverage of all available courses, but provides information from a range of both city and regional locations. While the information provided here is accurate at the time of printing, you should contact the universities for updated information, or check university websites for further courses.

Australian National University, Canberra ACT
*Contact:* Mr Tony Turner
General Inquiries: Undergraduate Administrator, Tel: (02) 6125 2723 Fax: 6125 4490 Email: schoolofhumanities@anu.edu.au
Website:www.arts.anu.edu.au/HSchool/humanities.htm
*Course Titles and Unit Titles:* Bachelor of Arts (Theatre Studies major)
*Auditions Required?* No.
*Experience Expected?* No specific requirements, but most units require a pass in practical and written components.
*Aims:* The essential aim of the Theatre Studies major is to provide students with 'knowledge about' theatre rather than teach 'skill in' theatre. As such Theatre Studies provides a part of a Liberal Arts education rather than a Professional Training.

Charles Sturt University, Wagga Wagga NSW
*Contact:* BA (Acting) Course Coordinator: John B Saunders
Tel: (02) 6933 2573 Fax: (02) 6933 2751; BA (Design) Course Coordinator: Kevin Poynter, Email: kpoynter@csu.edu au; Higher Degrees: Ray Goodlass, Tel: (02) 6933 2472 Fax (02) 6933 2887, Email: rgoodlass@csu.edu.au; Web: www.csu.edu.au
*Course Titles:* Bachelor of Arts (Acting for Screen & Stage); Bachelor of Arts (Acting for Screen & Stage); Bachelor of Arts

(Design for Theatre & Television); BA (Honours); MA in Visual and Performing Arts; MA Honours in Drama; PhD in Drama; Diploma in Education can also be studied after the BA for those who wish to teach drama in schools.

*Auditions Required?* Yes; applicants are required to attend an audition in Wagga Wagga (Riverina Playhouse) or Sydney (ATYP, Studio 2, The Wharf, Pier 4) in early December.

*Experience Expected?* No specific expectations, but the course gives as much weight to screen (television) acting as it does to stage.

*Aims:* It is a highly specialised course in acting for today's theatre and television industries. It is not a generalist drama course nor is it devoted to theoretical studies.

*How are Auditions Run?* Warm Up: the day will begin with a group warm up. Then you use your own relaxation and focussing techniques before presenting your monologues.

Most important—Two Compulsory Prepared Monologues: one classical and one modern from pieces specified by the University. Next in importance—Interview: you will be interviewed by the panel, including looking for applicants who understand the reality of the industry rather than have a 'starry-eyed' and naïve view of it. Group Improvisation: panel looks for spontaneity, inventiveness and creativity. Song Presentation: choose a song from the standard repertoire (from a musical). Own Choice Piece: you may be asked to present monologue of your own choice—a contrast to your compulsory monologues. Sight Reading: you may be asked to sight read a piece you have not previously seen. Auditions take the whole day: Warm Up; Compulsory Monologues until lunch. Afternoon call back for people successful so far for Song and Interview and perhaps other work. At the end of the day, depending on the number of applicants, we expect to indicate which applicants will be recommended to the University for an offer of a place.

*Any Other Information:* Students accepted for the course are required to provide their own makeup kit and a clothing kit specified by the University.

Deakin University, Melbourne Vic
*Contact:* Arts Faculty Office Tel: (03) 9244 3908 Fax 03 9244 6755
*Course Titles and Unit Titles:* Bachelor of Contemporary Arts; Bachelor of Arts; Applicants can apply to study drama or dance or both as part of either a BCA or BA degree
*Auditions Required?* Yes.
*Experience Expected?* No formal requirements.
*Aims:* The courses are included in a broader university education.
*How are Auditions Run?* Applicants are required to attend a half day audition consisting of workshops in improvisation, text and dance. Dance and drama applicants must attend both dance and drama auditions, but a poor showing in one area will not affect your chances of getting into the other. No memorising of speeches or other preparation is required, and no particular technique level is expected.
*Any Other Information:* The dance strand will sometimes select an applicant based on a video instead of a live audition.

Flinders University, Adelaide SA
*Contact:* Professor Julie Holledge, Director of the Drama Centre, Flinders University of South Australia, GPO Box 2100, Adelaide SA 5001. All enquiries to Anne Rizzo, Administrative Assistant, Drama Department, School of Humanities, Flinders University. Tel: (08) 8201 2631 Fax: (08) 8201 3635 Email: anne.rizzo@flinders.edu.au
*Course Titles and Unit Titles:* Bachelor of Creative Arts: Performance; Bachelor of Creative Arts: Direction; Drama Centre: Drama Centre is the four year specialist professional acting and directing training program. The acting course is equally divided between classes in live performance (theatre, physical theatre, cabaret) and electronic performance (film, video, digital animation). The directing course consists of classes in theatre, installation performance and design, and video. Students must direct a minimum of nine productions in the four years. All students take theory courses in modern and post-modern drama and take special studies in aspects of contemporary Australia,

European, Asian, or American theatre. Admission is strictly by audition held in November for the following year. You need to have passed the audition and have a Bachelor of Creative Arts (BCA) offer.

BA (Drama Major); BEd (Drama as teaching subject). In addition to the Drama Centre program, Flinders offers a Drama Major within the Bachelor of Arts. At first year level it is possible to take a simple audition (by improvisation) for Drama Workshop, and in later years, students can study Commedia dell'Arte and Stanislavsky. These topics enable you to nominate Drama as a teaching subject in a BEd. The very best students each year are also invited to audition for Drama Centre.

*Auditions Required?* Yes for Drama Centre (BCA) and a simplified theatre audition for Drama Workshop (BA)

*Experience Expected?* No formal requirements.

*Aims:* By deciding to train as a professional actor or director at Flinders you'll combine specialist practical training in your chosen area with a high quality education that teaches you about contemporary international performance on stage and screen. The aim of the course is to produce graduates qualified to work as independent artists across a variety of media, and capable of providing leadership within the performing arts.

*How are Auditions Run?* Entry by audition and interview. 12 performance students and 2 directing students selected annually. Performance. Day One: movement session; presentation of two monologues and one song; screen test. Day Two: movement class; presentation of material requested by audition panel on Day One; acting for camera audition; improvisation session. Day Three: interview and presentation of additional material. Directing. Day One: as for acting applicants. Day Two: Director's audition (this involves the applicant working with two of the Drama Centre actors on a scene selected by the panel); interview and presentation of additional material in video or written form that demonstrates the applicant's previous experience.

*Any Other Information:* Four year courses. The year is divided into four terms, in which students attend 15 hours of classes per week in acting or directing for theatre, television and film, and an additional 6 hours of lectures and seminars on theatre, film and television theory and history. Outside of the teaching terms, there are 3 production blocks of 5 weeks each, in which students rehearse full time and present theatre productions or complete the shooting of a video drama.

Griffith University, Brisbane Qld
*Contact:* Applied Theatre: Dr Tony Millett Tel (07) 3875 5672; Email t.millett@mailbox.gu.edu.au; Drama in Education: Dr Bruce Burton; Tel (07) 3875 5741; Email bruce.burton@mailbox.gu.edu.au; web www.gu.edu.au
*Course Titles and Unit Titles:* Bachelor of Arts (Applied Theatre); Bachelor of Education (Drama)
*Auditions Required?* Yes
*Experience Expected?* Contact the Course Convenors (above) if you have concerns.
*Aims:* Students enrolling in the four year BEd (Drama) will graduate as qualified secondary school teachers eligible to teach drama and one other subject area. The qualification is recognised nationally and internationally. The BA (Applied Theatre) is a three year course. Students have the option of an additional fourth honors year. This innovative course aims to develop articulate practitioners who are capable of applying theatre knowledge and skills in a wide variety of disparate fields including hospitality, tourism, broadcast journalism, habilitation and therapy, community cultural development, convention organisation and training contexts. In addition to theatre studies, students may therefore elect to undertake a second major from a range of options related to their chosen career interests.
*How are Auditions Run?* Applicants to both courses complete four tasks during a half-day audition process. Students are required to present, workshop and discuss one audition piece selected from the set pieces provided. The second task is a brief impromptu oral presentation. This is followed by a short 10 minute individual interview. This will include questions on drama experience, school achievements, projected subject exit levels, motives for studying drama at a tertiary level etc, as well as

addressing performance in the previous tasks. Applicants can expect to be asked about their audition piece and the play from which it comes. The final task is a previously unseen written task and requires no preparation.

La Trobe University, Melbourne Vic
*Contact:* Geoffrey Milne; Email: G.Milne@latrobe.edu.au
*Course Titles and Unit Titles:* Bachelor of Arts; Bachelor of Creative Arts (from 2003)
*Auditions Required?* No
*Experience Expected?* Entry is by TER (ENTRY) score and interview, conducted at the point of enrolment.
*Aims:* We are not a performing arts vocational training institution. The Theatre and Drama Program at La Trobe University is part of the School of Communication, Arts & Critical Enquiry.
*Any Other Information:* Details of the new BCA course are available from the University.

The National Theatre, Melbourne Vic
*Contact:* The Administrator, National Theatre Drama School, PO Box 1173, St Kilda South, Vic, 3182. Tel: (03) 9534 0223 Fax (03) 9534 5345
*Course Titles:* Three Year Acting Course for people over the age of 20 who wish to be professional Actors; One Year Music Theatre Course for people over the age of 18 years; also Workshop Classes for people 18 years and over.
*Auditions Required?* For Acting Course and Musical Theatre: Audition, Interview and Fees on application.
*Experience Expected?* No formal requirements, but high expectations.
*Aims:* Acting Course: First Year classes are across 4 terms, on Monday, Tuesday and Thursday nights – 7.00 p.m. – 10.00 p.m. Focus is on skills development in Acting, Movement and Voice, with regular specific projects and a Theatre Exercise at the end of Term 4 in the Studio Theatre. Second Year students study a minimum of three nights a week with significant increase in

hours during productions. Specialist workshops continue in acting and skills development with a Term 4 production in the Studio Theatre. Third Year students study four nights a week concentrating on 2 major public productions (one with a guest Director), Film and Television techniques, Audition, and Performance Making. Students successfully completing Third Year appear in the Industry Showcase to which the National Theatre invites agents, casting directors and other industry representatives. All tutors are trained working professionals, and there are frequent showings of work and ongoing assessments throughout the year. Students are invited to continue training at the discretion of the Director of Drama.

Music Theatre: The curriculum includes intensive acting, singing and dance training – and also covers related subjects such as music theory, audition techniques, song repertoire and music theatre history. Applicants are expected to continue they external singing tuition. Students receive expert vocal coaching from staff and participate in masterclasses given by guest lecturers. Our students are challenged to move beyond the Presentational performance style often associated with this genre. Music theatre students who have completed the course and reached a level of skill deemed to be of Industry Standard are invited to appear in the Showcase.

*How are Auditions Run?* Acting Course: Applicants must prepare two contrasting Classical and contemporary text based monologues. They will audition for the Director of Drama and teaching staff of the school. All other applicants on that day are in the room, and they will be taken through a 15 minute warm up by staff prior to their audition to help focus and steady them. They can choose the order of presenting, each person offers the first piece, followed by a brief group time out and warm up for the second piece. Lines must be learned. No self-devised work will be accepted. No feedback will be offered. Outstanding applicants may be asked to work with the staff, and to undergo a personal interview. They are then told if they have been selected for the Call Back Workshop, and what additional preparation may be required. The Call Back Workshop is 3 hours and

includes vocal and physical warm ups, improvisation, and exercises designed to show the students' abilities to demonstrate a flexible approach, openness to working in a group, and response to input and direction. Successful students are notified in writing of the offer of a place in the course.
Music Theatre: Audition comprises two contrasting songs and a monologue followed by a dance call back.
*Any other Information:* The National Theatre Drama School is not covered by Austudy.

National Institute of Dramatic Art (NIDA)
University of New South Wales, Sydney, NSW 2052
*Contact:* The Admissions Officer; Tel: (02) 9697 7600, web www.nida.unsw.edu.au
*Aim:* To provide exceptionally talented young people with a range of vocational skills and to assist them to apply these skills with imagination and intelligence to the realities of working careers in professional theatre, film and television; as actors, stage managers, designers, directors and crafts people.
*Course Titles and Unit Titles:* Bachelor of Dramatic Art in Acting; Design; Technical Production; and Production Crafts; specialising in Properties or Costumes; Graduate Diploma of Dramatic Art in Voice Studies, Movement Studies, Directing; Advanced Diploma of Dramatic Art in Scenery Construction.
*Auditions Required:* Yes
*Requirements for admission:* Admission requirements are included in the prospectus available from the Admissions Officer or off the NIDA website.
*Experience Expected:* The primary criterion for admission is evidence of the applicant's talent, aptitude, ability enthusiasm and commitment in the entertainment industry.
*How are Auditions Run:* Applicants for the Bachelor of Dramatic Art in Acting must attend an audition. Applicants for all other courses will be required to attend an interview. Other prerequisites are outlined in the current prospectus. Applicants will be told on the day of audition if they are required for a second audition or interview or if their application has been

unsuccessful. Successful applicants will be offered a place at NIDA by telephone and by letter before the end of December.
*Any Other Information:* Applications are accepted from 1st July, closing on the 31st October of the same year; in some cases late applications are accepted. The NIDA Open Program provides access to performing arts training for the community at large through short, non-accredited practical courses in theatre, film and televisions. The courses cover acting, directing, design, costume making, video, playwriting, theatre technology and production skills. Courses are available not only at NIDA in Sydney, but in other capital cities and territories, and in regional areas across Australia. Many of the courses are directly aimed at youth and include: The Breakfast Club - Drama classes for young people 3 - 17 years; Studio Two - A part-time Acting Course for young people 15 - 17 years; Special Workshop Series - Specialised workshops designed to extend and challenge participants working knowledge of theatre, film and television; School Holiday Workshops - A series of exciting workshop covering many aspects of film theatre and television. For more information please contact: NIDA Open Program on (02) 9697 7626 or the NIDA website: www.nida.edu.au

Queensland University of Technology
Kelvin Grove, Brisbane Qld
*Contact:* John O'Hare, Head Acting & Technical Production Department, Faculty of Arts, Queensland University of Technology, Kelvin Grove Campus, Victoria Park Road, Kelvin Grove Qld 4059; Tel: (07) 3864 5998; Fax: 3864 3672; John O'Hare academy@qut.edu.au
*Course Titles:* Bachelor of Fine Arts: BFA (Acting); BFA (Technical Production)
*Auditions Required?* Yes for Acting. Interview only for Technical.
*Experience Expected?* No formal requirements, but previous experience an advantage, especially for BFA Technical Production.
*Aims:* Both Acting and Technical Production strands of this department are strongly vocational in nature. They offer

intensive, conservatory style training programs. Students graduating from these two programs are trained to a skill level that prepares them to move directly into the Performing Arts profession. Students in this department are expected to demonstrate an extremely high standard and work ethic and commitment in order to retain their place in the course.

*How are Auditions Run?* Applicants are required to learn two monologues of their own choice or from the list of suggested speeches. The applicant will present their piece, after which the audition panel will take the applicant through some improvisation and directorial approaches to the piece. This completes the first round of assessment for that applicant. We then do a round of callbacks, only for applicants who were successful in the first round. A more rigorous nuts and bolts approach to the applicant's instrumental blocks and tensions (voice, body mask, emotional range) is assessed in the callback sessions. This takes more time per applicant as we are looking for specific and individual potentialities. If the applicant is successful in the callbacks they will be interviewed to assess the practicalities of the applicant's position should they be offered a place in the Acting Studio.

*Any Other Information:* Students should expect flexible scheduling in the timetable and an altered University timetable of semesters and vacations. Oodgeroo Unit: This student support unit aims to develop and improve access, participation and successful outcomes for Aboriginal and Torres Strait Islander students.

University of Ballarat, Ballarat Vic
*Contact:* Kim Durban, Arts Academy, Camp St Arts Precinct, University of Ballarat. Postal Address: PO Box 745, Ballarat 3353, Tel: (03) 5333 3537 Email: k.durban@ballarat.edu.au Website: www.ballarat.edu.au/arts/bapa
*Course Titles:* Bachelor of Arts (Theatre Performance); Bachelor of Arts (Theatre Production); Bachelor of Arts (Music Theatre Performance)
*Auditions Required?* Yes, for Theatre Performance and Musical Theatre. Entry to Theatre Production is by interview.

*Experience Expected?* No formal requirements.
*Aims:* The Theatre Performance degree offers focussed theatre study, allowing students to develop their skills and gain the techniques needed to become a professional actor. The course is underpinned by a philosophy of blending practice with theory, incorporating workshops, rehearsal and research, and is delivered by respected artists and teachers, ensuring that the perspective gained by emerging performers is relevant, rigorous and contemporary. The Theatre Production degree offers a realistic approach to the complex environment of professional backstage work, placing emphasis on autonomy, initiative and leadership skills. The Music Theatre Performance degree seeks to develop multi-skilled performers for professional music theatre. Students are encouraged to create new work and explore the history and theoretical base of contemporary music theatre.
*How are Auditions Run?* Acting: Two contrasting monologues, one classical, one contemporary. A callback in group and ensemble improvisation, movement and voice. Music Theatre: two songs, one up tempo and one ballad, and a monologue. A callback in dance skills. Production: a model for a set project. All courses: an interview regarding previous interest / experience in theatre and ambitions for training.
*Any Other Information:* Students work to a high standard and are expected to apply a professional level of discipline and commitment. The course is now located at a $27 million arts precinct in the heart of Ballarat.

University of Melbourne, Melbourne Vic
Note: This is not the Victorian College of the Arts (VCA) course
*Contact:* Theatre Studies Coordinator: Dr Peter Eckersall, School of Creative Arts, Tel (03) 8344 8627 Fax (03) 8344 8462 Email eckersal@unimelb.edu.au. Post Graduate Studies Coordinator: Dr Denise Varney, School of Creative Arts
Tel (03) 8344 8579 Fax (03) 8344 8462 Email dvarney@unimelb.edu.au
*Course Titles and Unit Titles:* Bachelor of Creative Arts; Bachelor of Creative Arts Honours; Graduate Diploma in Creative Arts;

Master of Creative Arts (by research); Doctor of Philosophy.
*Auditions Required?* No.
*Experience Expected?* None assumed. Entry by Tertiary Entrance Rank (TER). For details of entry see: www.sca.unimelb.edu.au
*Aims:* The Theatre Studies program at the University of Melbourne is an integrated theory-practice study offering subjects across a spectrum of performance modalities and includes studies in European, Greek, Japanese and Australian theatre, feminist theatre, contemporary theatre production, modern, postmodern and postcolonial theatre studies, and technology and performance art. In the undergraduate degree students are offered subjects tending towards the theatre and performance studies disciplines. Students in the Bachelor of Creative Arts who major in theatre studies do so as part of an interdisciplinary degree that also offers studies in visual and media arts and creative writing. The University of Melbourne also has a varied and active student theatre scene where many of Australia's most innovative theatre artists first practised their craft. The Master of Creative Arts and Doctor of Philosophy offer advanced research, a component of which can be undertaken by practice. The theatre studies area in the school has a staff of four: Dr Denise Varney, Paul Monaghan, Associate Professor Angela O'Brien, Dr Peter Eckersall and a lively mix of sessional staff and post-graduate students. Theatre Studies does not offer the vocational training of actors, directors or designers. Rather the program takes responsibility for the investigation of theatre as a historical, cultural and aesthetic form which has been a dynamic art form across cultures since the beginnings of recorded time.

University of New England, Armidale NSW
*Contact:* Professor Adrian Kiernander, Theatre Studies, School of English, Communication and Theatre Tel: 02 6773 2534 Fax: 02 6773 2623 Email: akiernan@metz.une.edu.au
Web www.une.edu.au/theatre-studies
*Course Title:* Bachelor of Arts (Theatre)
*Auditions Required?* No.

*Experience Expected?* No previous experience necessary. Desirable attributes are enthusiasm, dedication and reliability.
*Aims:* The aims of the course are to give students knowledge about theatre, to prepare them to be better performers, more informed audiences, or as generic skills for careers involving dealing with the public and live oral presentation. We are not an actor-training school, though there are many practical theatre skills that are taught and developed in the course. There is a practical course in directing in which all students direct a production of their choice. There are 4 or 5 formal contact hours a week for each unit of study, but students are required to spend approximately 10 hours a week including preparation and rehearsal. For students involved in optional major productions the rehearsal time increases. Some of our graduates apply for specific vocational training in theatre on completion of the course. A small number go directly into work as theatre practitioners. Others move into the area of teaching, especially secondary school drama teaching, and some continue with study to postgraduate level.

University of Southern Queensland, Toowoomba, Qld.
*Contact:* Ms Cheryl Kanowski, Department of Theatre, University of Southern Queensland, Toowoomba 4350, Tel (07) 4631 1121 Fax (07) 4631 1133, Email kanowski@usq.edu.au Web www.usq.edu.au/faculty/arts/theatre/arthead.htm
*Course Title*: Bachelor of Theatre Arts
*Auditions Required?* Acting yes. Stage Management and Technical Production: Project presentation and interview; Drama and Theatre Studies: Project presentation and interview.
*Experience Expected?* Contact the University about details of projects to be presented for Technical Production and Theatre Studies.
*Aims:* Acting and Stage Management and Technical Production: Each course provides students with a comprehensive base of professional skills and education standards required for entry into the entertainment industries. Drama and Theatre Studies: graduates from this course possess skills formative to building careers as writers, dramaturgs, community arts officers, arts administrators, teachers and academics.

*How are Auditions Run?* For Acting: auditions include group work, pair work, improvisation, monologue, singing, call back and interview. Stage Management and Technical Production, and Drama and Theatre Studies: a project and interview are required.
*Any Other Information:* The USQ Theatre Department has a long history of involvement with training foreign students for the performance industries. Students from outside Australia wishing to enquire about special audition / interview arrangements should contact Head, Department of Theatre (Tel 07 4631 1123, email foy@usq.edu.au).

University of Tasmania, Launceston Tas
*Contact:* Associate Professor John Lohrey, Deputy Head, School of Visual and Performing Arts, Locked Bag 1 - 362, University of Tasmania, Launceston Tas 7250, Tel: (03) 6324 4400 Fax: (03) 6324 4401 Email: J.Lohrey@utas.edu.au
*Course Titles :* Bachelor of Contemporary Arts (Theatre)
*Auditions Required?* Yes for acting. Interview and folio for other areas.
*Experience Expected?* No formal requirements.
*Aims:* The program offers intending professionals the opportunity to pursue specifically focussed studies, designed to equip graduates with the skills to enter the theatre industry as either performers or technicians. It also caters for those wishing to become teachers and for those who seek to develop theatre skills for use in a community setting.
Career Opportunities: Graduates of the School have secured employment in theatre companies, in acting, technical and administrative roles, as well as in television and radio, the music industry and theatre-in-education. Some graduates go on to take a Bachelor of Teaching while qualified graduates will have the opportunity to proceed to study for honours or a higher degree.
*How are Auditions Run?* Acting auditions involve: monologue; descriptive prose; students' own creative material eg music, dance etc; theatre review; interview.
*Any Other Information:* Weekly contact: 16 hours with additional commitments outside class time to rehearsals, projects and

preparation. Students will follow either performance or technical theatre. While allowing for individual student choice in the latter stages, the course is intentionally broadly based and reflects an eclectic approach to both theories of acting and all styles and forms of theatrical expression.

University of Wollongong, Wollongong NSW
*Contact:* Jeff Kevin, Coordinator Performance,
Faculty of Creative Arts, University of Wollongong, Wollongong NSW 2522, Tel: (02) 4221 3583 Fax: (02) 4221 3301 Email: jeff_kevin@uow.edu.au
*Course Titles:* Bachelor of Creative Arts (Performance)
*Auditions Required?* Yes.
*Experience Expected?* No formal requirements.
*Aims:* Seminars addressing all aspects of performance will provide students with the opportunity to perform for their peers and for visiting professional artists in masterclass and workshop situations. Towards the end of their training students are introduced to the industry, either at the University or at a venue in Sydney, where they perform from a repertoire of selected works developed over the course of their degree.
*How are Auditions Run?* Structure of Audition Day (for acting): The morning focuses on two aspects of the applicant's work—their participation and interaction in group warm-up exercises, and their ability to interpret a set text and song. (This individual audition is closed to all but staff.) The afternoon focusses on flexibility and whether the candidate can adapt to new stimulus, such as re-direction and improvisation. (This part of the audition is viewed by all applicants on that day with the exception of the final interview.) Structure of the Audition Day (for other areas): The audition begins with an introduction and group warm up. This warm up consists of physical and vocal exercises. Applicants should be aware that both the ability to sing and dance are looked for in this period. Each applicant then presents his or her individual work (either a monologue or scene plus a song of their own choice) to the audition panel. A campus tour is provided during the lunch break. The second part of the day begins with a series of group improvisations chosen by

participating staff and are designed to observe the applicant's ability at devising new work, and for observing interaction between individuals in the group. Each applicant performs aspects of their individual work for re-direction and critical feedback. Finally, all applicants are given a final interview.

Victorian College of the Arts (VCA)
(University of Melbourne), Melbourne Vic.
*Contact:* The Drama School Administration, Victorian College of the Arts, School of Drama, 234 St Kilda Road, Southbank Vic 3006. Tel: (03) 9685 9325 Fax: (03) 9685 9462 Email: drama.info@vca.unimelb.edu.au Web: www.vca.unimelb.edu.au
*Course Titles:* Bachelor of Dramatic Art – Acting. Also available for applicants who already hold a tertiary qualification or have relevant experience: Graduate Diploma of Dramatic Art (Directing); Graduate Diploma in Animateuring; Master of Dramatic Art (Directing); Master of Animateuring.
*Auditions Required?* Yes.
*Experience Expected?* No formal requirements.
*Aims:* The philosophy and practice of the School of Drama recognises that the training of artists needs to occur within an atmosphere of permission where investigation and learning are inextricably fused. Our school trains independent artists with a passion for theatre and a desire to contribute in a meaningful way to its evolution. The making of new work is consequently an integral part of the course. Our approach is based on a fundamental respect for the ethics of theatre practice.
*How are Auditions Run?* All audition applicants are asked to prepare two audition monologues, one classical and one contemporary, from the VCA Audition booklet. The auditions are conducted by two auditioners. They begin with current students taking the group of 15-20 auditionees through a physical and vocal warm-up. Each auditionee will then perform one of their monologues in front of the group. The auditioners will stipulate whether it is to be the classical or the contemporary piece first. After a break, each participant will then perform their second monologue to the group. The auditionees are then asked to wait outside as the auditioners confer. This is the end of the

first phase of the audition process.

The group is then informed if the auditioners require any participants to stay for more intense work. Further work will consist of re-working the audition speeches, impulse work on the floor and an interview. The auditionee will then be informed whether they are invited to return for a call back. The call back may involve any or all of the following: preparing and presenting an alternative speech; presenting the same speeches again; being re-directed; physical and vocal impulse work; and working with the other auditionees in pairs or groups.

*Any Other Information:* The Bachelor of Dramatic Art is a three-year intensive actor training program, where the student actor is equipped to meet the challenge of developing a methodology which enables them to work in any professional theatre, film and television context. The goal of the training is to provide the student with techniques which will allow them to transform into a variety of complex characters through emotional, vocal and physical fluency, in the context of scripted work. The training is intense and all consuming. Students must attend classes and rehearsals from 9 to 6 daily and will be expected to be available for rehearsal and personal project group work after hours and on weekends. Students are not allowed to audition for, or perform in, any performance outside the school during their course of study. Assessment is rigorous throughout the course. Those who reach graduation are launched into the industry by means of a Performance Day where students showcase their skills to an audience of agents and industry professionals.

Western Australian Academy of Performing Arts (WAAPA) (Edith Cowan University), Perth WA
Contact: James Hamilton, Admissions Officer, Western Australian Academy of Performing Arts, 2 Bradford St, Mt Lawley WA 6050, Tel: (08) 9370 6594 Fax: (08) 9370 6665
Website: www.waapa.cowan.edu.au
*Course Titles and Unit Titles:* Advanced Diploma of Performing Arts (Acting); Bachelor of Arts (Broadcasting); Bachelor of Arts (Musical Theatre); Certificate II in Musical Theatre; Certificate III in Theatre (Aboriginal)

*Auditions Required?* Yes and Tertiary Entrance Rank (TER) for Bachelors. Year 10 assumed for Certificate Courses.
Technical courses require interview and submission of a project.
*Experience Expected?* No formal requirements.
*Aims:* WAAPA performance and technical courses are highly vocational in nature. There is a large number of contact hours per week and these hours increase over a five week production cycle. WAAPA courses are Austudy approved, yet the workload limits opportunity for casual work. In other words the students need financial backing prior to coming in to the course. The expectation is that the course will be the students' sole priority and focus while at WAAPA. In spite of this institutional ethos and perhaps because of it, there is a very strong sense of community at WAAPA where staff and students have close relationships. Another factor is that many of our students come from interstate to study.
*How are Auditions Run?* Actors: Auditions are held Australia-wide during November/December. Applicants are required to perform two pieces for a panel selected from a list provided, one from a 20th century text and one from Shakespeare in verse. International students may apply by video. Music Theatre: Auditions are held Australia wide during November and December. Applicants are required to perform two songs of contrasting style, both of which must be from the musical theatre repertoire and must be performed with accompaniment, plus one monologue from a list provided. Applicants may also be asked to return for a group class to ascertain aptitude for dance training. Overseas applicants may apply by video.
*Any Other Information:* WAAPA also offers courses in broadcasting; dance; classical, jazz and contemporary music; and fine arts. It is a very broad based arts community and students benefit from interaction with artists from other areas.
Notification of acceptance into the course will be given by early December. You must confirm by fax or post within 3 days of receiving the notification whether you wish to take up the offer. Failure to do this could mean that the place is offered to someone on the reserve list.

# REFERENCES
## PRINT
Allen, Richard James & Pearlman, Karen (eds.) *performing the unNameable* Sydney: Currency Press, 1999.

*Australasian Drama Studies* St Lucia, Qld: Department of English, University of Queensland (1982 - )

Beckett, Samuel. *Waiting for Godot.* London: Faber & Faber, 1956.

Benedetti, Robert L. *The Actor at Work*. Englewood Cliffs: Prentice-Hall, 1986.

Benedetti, Robert L. *The Director at Work*. Englewood Cliffs: Prentice-Hall, 1985.

Berkoff, Steven. *Free Association* (autobiography). London: Faber and Faber, 1997.

———. *Plays 1*: *East, West, Greek, Sink the Belgrano!, Massage, Lunch, The Bow of Ulysses, Sturm und Drang*. London: Faber and Faber, 2000.

———.*Plays 2: Decadence, Kvetch, Acapulco, Harry's Christmas, Brighton Beach Scumbags, Darling You Were Marvellous, Pitbull, Actor*. London: Faber and Faber, 1996.

———. *Plays 3: Rtiual in Blood, Messiah, Oedipus*. London: Faber and Faber, 2000.

Brecht, Bertolt. *The Caucasian Chalk Circle*. London: Methuen, 1984.

———.*The Threepenny Opera* London: Eyre Methuen, 1973.

———.*Mother Courage and Her Children*. London: Methuen, 1962.

———.*Life of Galileo*. London: Methuen, 1980.

Brockett, Oscar. *The Theatre: An Introduction*. New York: Holt, Rinehart and Winston, 1969.

Buzo, Alex. *Coralie Lansdowne Says No* Sydney: Currency Press, 1974.

Carey, Dean. *Masterclass Vols I & II* Sydney: Currency Press, 1995.

Chekov, Anton. *The Seagull, and other plays*. Melbourne: Penguin, 1954.

De Groen, Alma. *The Girl Who Saw Everything*. Sydney: Currency Press, 1993.

———. *The Joss Adams Show*. Sydney: Currency Press, 1977.

———. *The Rivers of China*. Sydney: Currency Press, 1988.

———. *Vocations and Going Home*. Sydney: Currency Press, 1983.

Dunmore, Simon. *Alternative Shakespeare Auditions*. Sydney: Currency Press, 1998.

Earley, Michael & Keil, Philippa. *Solo! The best Monologues of the 80s*. New York: Applause 1989.

Earley, Michael & Keil, Philippa. *The Modern Monologue*. London: Methuen, 1993.

Eliot, T.S. *Murder in the Cathedral*. London: Faber and Faber, 1968.

Esslin, Martin (ed.) *Illustrated Encyclopaedia of World Theatre*. London: Thames & Hudson, 1977.

Gascoigne, Bamber. *World Theatre: An Illustrated History*. London: Ebury Press, 1968.1968.

Gordon, Hayes. *Acting and Performing* Sydney: Ensemble Press, 1992.

Hewett, Dorothy. *The Chapel Perilous*. Sydney: Currency Press, 1977.

Holloway, Peter. *Contemporary Australian Drama*. Sydney: Currency Press, 1981.

Ibsen, Henrik trans. Peter Watts. *A Doll's House*. London: Penguin 1965.

Irvin, Eric. *Theatre Comes to Australia*. St Lucia: University of Queensland Press, 1971.

John, Rosemary. *Luck of the Draw*. Sydney: Currency Press, 1986.

Kenna, Peter. *Furtive Love*. Sydney: Currency Press, 1980.

Kohlhaas, Karen. *The Monologue Audition: A Practical Guide for Actors*. New York: Limelight, 2000.

Miller, Arthur. *After the Fall*. New York: Viking Press, 1968.

Molinari, Cesare. *Theatre Through the Ages*. London: Cassell 1975.

Nowra, Louis. *Capricornia*. Sydney: Currency Press, 1988.

———. *Cosi*. Sydney: Currency Press, 1992.

———. *Crow*. Sydney: Currency Press, 1990.

———.*The Golden Age*. Sydney: Currency Press, 1985.

———.*The Incorruptible*. Sydney: Currency Press, 1995.

———.*Inner Voices/Albert Names Edward*. Sydney: Currency Press, 1983.

———.*Inside the Island/The Precious Woman*. Sydney: Currency Press, 1981.

———.*Radiance*. Sydney: Currency Press, 2000.

———. *Summer Of The Aliens*. Sydney: Currency Press, 1992.

O'Neill, Eugene. *Mourning Becomes Electra*. London: Jonathan Cape, 1932.

Radic, Leonard. *The State of Play – The Revolution in the Australian Theatre since the 1960s*. Ringwood: Penguin, 1991.

Shakespeare, William. *Complete Works of William Shakespeare*. London: Murrays, nd.

Shaw, George Bernard. *Standard Edition of the Works of Bernard Shaw: Pygmalion; My Fair Lady; Mrs Warren's Profession; Heartbreak House; St Joan; Arms and the Man*. London: Constable & Company 1932.

Stanislavsky, Konstantin. *An Actor Prepares*. London: Methuen, 1980.

———. *Building a Character*. London: Methuen, 1979.

———. *Creating a Role*. London: Methuen, 1980.

Stewart, Douglas. *Fire on the Snow*. Sydney: Angus & Robertson, 1944.

Styan J.L. *Modern Drama in Theory and Practice*. Cambridge: Cambridge University Press, 1981.

West, John. *Theatre in Australia*. Sydney: Cassell, 1978.

Williamson, David. *Brilliant Lies*. Sydney: Currency Press, 1993.

———. *Dead White Males*. Sydney: Currency Press, 1995.

———. *Don's Party*. Sydney: Currency Press, 1995.

———. *Jack Manning Trilogy: Face to Face, Charitable Intent, A Conversation*. Sydney: Currency Press, 2002.

———. *The Removalist*. Sydney: Currency Press, 1972.

## ORGANISATIONS & WEB PAGES

Australian Broadcasting Corporation (ABC) (2000) SeaChange

Australian National Playwrights' Centre (ANPC)

Government Agencies - See Government websites: www.fed.gov.au (Australian Tax Office; Centrelink; Arts Council; Workplace Agreements; Human Rights and Equal Opportunity Commission) www.wa.gov.au www.sa.gov.au www.nt.gov.au www.vic.gov.au www.tas.gov.au www.act.gov.au www.qld.gov.au www.nsw.gov.au (arts administration and funding at state level; state industrial courts; state and local libraries; permit authorities - eg permits for performing in specific locations, using weapons on stage)

Media & Entertainment Alliance of Australia (MEAA)
For membership inquiries 1300 65 65 13

Theatresports®: International Theatresports Institute website: www.intl-theatresports.ab.ca; postal address: P.O. Box 82084, 1400 - 12 Ave. S.W., Calgary, AB, T3C 3W5, Canada. Email: admin@intl-theatresports.ab.ca

Virtual Library of Theatre and Drama: www.vl-theatre.com